Drama Lessons: Ages 4–7

Designed for busy teachers, *Drama Lessons: Ages 4–7* provides tried and tested lesson plans which will help you to make your drama lessons fun learning experiences. *Drama Lessons: Ages 4–7* emerges from the continuing positive responses to *Drama Lessons for Five to Eleven Year Olds* (2001) and the three book series, *Role Play in The Early Years* (2004). In this book you will find a carefully chosen selection of the best lessons taken from these four texts, plus some exciting new material – a combination of brand new and classic lessons. This new collection introduces *Literacy Alerts* which identify how the drama activities develop aspects of literacy and suggest additional literacy activities.

For each lesson plan, essential resources and timing information are provided. The lessons cover a range of themes and curriculum areas. Specialists and non-specialists, nursery nurses, teaching assistants and playgroup leaders will find the book easy to use and it will give all trainee teachers a flying start in their school placements.

Judith Ackroyd is Dean of the Faculty of Humanities, Arts and Social Sciences at Regent's College, London.

Jo Barter-Boulton is Senior Lecturer in the School of Education at the University of Northampton.

Drama Lessons:
Ages 4–7

Second Edition

Judith Ackroyd and
Jo Barter-Boulton

Routledge
Taylor & Francis Group

LONDON AND NEW YORK

First published as *Drama Lessons for Five to Eleven year olds* 2001
by David Fulton Publishers
This second edition published 2013
by Routledge
2 Park Square, Milton Park, Abingdon, Oxon OX14 4RN

Simultaneously published in the USA and Canada
by Routledge
711 Third Avenue, New York, NY 10017

Routledge is an imprint of the Taylor & Francis Group, an informa business

British Library Cataloguing in Publication Data
A catalogue record for this book is available from the British Library

Library of Congress Cataloguing in Publication Data
A catalog record for this book has been requested

ISBN: 978-0-415-51697-6 (pbk)
ISBN: 978-0-203-12160-3 (ebk)

Typeset in Helvetica by Fakenham Prepress Solutions, Fakenham, Norfolk NR21 8NN

Printed and bound in Great Britain by the MPG Books Group

Contents

Acknowledgements

We wish to thank the teachers, students and colleagues who have excited us with their drama work for children. Thanks also to those who have helped shape our own practice over many years: Gavin Bolton, David Booth, Dorothy Heathcote, Carole Miller, Jonothan Neelands, Cecily O'Neil, John O'Toole, Juliana Saxton and Philip Taylor. Bruce Roberts and James Hobbs at Routledge have been a delight to work with – we are most grateful. We are indebted to our artists, Charlie, Tobias, Rupert, Phoebe and Beth.

Introduction

This book emerges from the warm reaction to *Drama Lessons for Five to Eleven Year Olds* published in 2001 and the three books in the *Role Play in the Early Years* series published in 2004. These were written in response to the interest of teachers and students who were keen to use drama in their teaching and wanted more user-friendly material. Rather than simply producing a second edition of *Drama Lessons for Five to Eleven Year Olds*, we wished to produce two distinctive age-specific texts to ensure teachers get more appropriate material for their book/buck! Hence, in addition to this book, *Drama Lessons: Ages 4–7*, there is a sister text, *Drama Lessons: Ages 7–11*.

Again, we have chosen to concentrate purely on drama lesson plans rather than theorizing drama practice. A selection of useful publications is listed at the back of this book. The two new books feature some old favourites from the published four books alongside some previously unpublished materials. We are writing primarily for those teachers who have had little or no experience of teaching drama, but who have an interest in the subject and a willingness to have a go at lessons devised, tried and tested by other teachers. Experienced teachers may appreciate some new materials to add to their repertoire.

The dramas in this book are designed to fulfil a range of learning objectives in various curriculum areas and develop particular literacy skills through a creative curriculum approach. All dramas feature *Literacy Alerts*, which are identified by these icons: and to highlight opportunities for literacy learning. We have focused on *Literacy Alerts* as we want to foreground the importance of drama as a way of developing and enriching literacy skills across the primary curriculum. This icon identifies the literacy skills being developed by the drama activity. This icon identifies suggestions for additional literacy work that can be developed from the dramas.

The book provides all the information necessary for teachers to pick up and teach, with the authorial voice speaking directly to you, the teacher. Dramatic approaches are explained as they are used in the chapters. In addition, a glossary with instructions for a few useful drama games are provided. The resources required are listed and estimated timings for each lesson are given. These times cannot be exact because different children respond differently to the same stimuli, and therefore an activity can take as much as thirty minutes more with one group than another.

Each drama is made up of a sequence of activities, most of which need to be followed in the order given. We are aware that teachers are working in different spaces with different children and with different constraints. The book is therefore designed so that teachers can do as much or as little of the drama at any one time as is appropriate. Sometimes teachers may choose to include fifteen minutes of drama activity in a group session while others may choose to teach a whole drama during a half-day session.

We are delighted to have been given the opportunity to share more drama adventures with you and your children.

Teachers' notes

The layout of the book

Each plan is introduced with the following:

- **A brief synopsis** – a few lines outlining the story.
- **Learning objectives** – key areas we want children to know or understand by the end of the lesson. These are cross curricular and are not exhaustive. Many specific literacy learning moments are identified elsewhere in the Literacy Alerts (see below).
- **Themes** – again, these are cross curricular.
- **Resources** – provides a list of what you will need to deliver the lesson.
- **Timing** – suggested timings for the drama if the lesson was taught in one session. All groups are different and some teachers may choose to do only one short activity at a time. This may depend on the age of the children, their experience of drama and the organization of the school day.

The lesson plans are then divided into sections. Each section includes the following:

- **Teacher's intentions** – these explain the thinking behind the drama activity selected.
- **Type of activity** – explains what the children will be doing.

- **Literacy Alerts** – these *Literacy Alerts* highlight very specific literacy learning that should take place during the drama activity, e.g. prediction. This symbol highlights additional literacy activities which may take place before, during or even after the drama. These are not essential for teaching the main drama.

- **Reflection activities** – at the end of each lesson we have included opportunities for the children to reflect on what they have learned through the drama. These reflection activities may be through further drama work or through questions and discussion.

Delivering the dramas

Teacher in role
The dramas included in this book engage the teacher working in role. This does *not* mean that you have to use exaggerated voices or funny walks. Costumes and props are not necessary, although we provide suggestions of what might be used to help the children to distinguish between you as the teacher and you in role. It is important that you make it very clear when you are in role to avoid confusion. A hat can be quickly put on and taken off when you move between teacher and role, for example. All the teacher roles can be male or female, so you can change the names if you like, or you can play a different gender.

Choosing the drama activities appropriate for your class

All these dramas could be used across the 4–7 age range. The more the children partic-ipate in drama activities, the more comfortable and confident they will become.

Some of the games described on page xvi are specifically used in these dramas because they develop relevant skills. However, these games can all be used indepen-dently. Many teachers like to play a game prior to starting their dramas.

Preparing to teach

It is essential to read the lesson plan all the way through before starting. This will enable you to prepare the space and any required resources. You may also wish to select any of the additional literacy activities indicated by the icon .

The plans can be adapted if you feel that you would like to give more time to some activities or place more emphasis on some of the sections. You may choose to do just one activity for a few minutes.

Once you have used some of the dramatic activities through teaching the lessons provided, you may wish to select some from the Glossary to use in your own planning. You may also like to look at the other drama books recommended at the back of the book, which will give you more ideas.

Before starting you may wish to agree a signal with the children which you will use to gain their attention, such as a hand raised, or a countdown: *3, 2, 1, freeze!*

Introducing teacher roles

In some of these dramas we use a bag of clothing and props to introduce each new teacher role. This is a really good way to build up a picture of each character before the teacher 'becomes' him or her in the drama. It is important to choose a suitable bag for each role and carefully select a few appropriate items of clothing or props. Children are extremely good at reading signs, therefore be careful not to give a wrong impression of the role by choosing inappropriate clothing for it. You need to decide what impression you want the children to get and paint a clear picture so there is no confusion. For example, if you want a character to be a more traditional older lady, perhaps choose a wicker basket and a floral scarf rather than a plastic carrier bag and a leather jacket. However, you may decide that she is a very trendy lady and would be very comfortable in a leather jacket and a motorbike helmet. By revealing one thing from the bag at a time, suspense is built up, and the children can offer their ideas about what they think the person is going to be like.

If you don't want to use props and costumes it is still possible to introduce the role by simply saying, 'In the next part of the story I am going to be ...'

The imaginative play area

The drama you choose to do with your children could be one which links to your imagi-native play area. We have included some simple design ideas for imaginative play areas which link directly to our dramas.

Glossary

The glossary of the dramatic terms used in this book is not necessary to teach the activities in these chapters, since each activity is fully explained in the text. However, the glossary provides explanations of a range of the dramatic approaches used in the book and may help those who, having used them in these dramas, wish to plan their own drama sessions. We hope therefore that our notes on what the different activities can achieve and why we might choose to use them might be helpful.

Collective drawing and map making

Individuals add detail to a picture or map. Children come forward one or two at a time and draw on to the basic outline, which has been prepared by the teacher. Sometimes it will be quicker to give each child a piece of paper or a post-it note on which to draw. These individual drawings can then be stuck on to the outline picture. Alternatively, groups might be given parts of a complete picture or map to work on. These are then brought together to create one large illustration that all children have contributed to. This way of working gives the finished product collective ownership. If time is restricted, the picture can be finished later.

Collective or collaborative storytelling

The whole class joins in with the telling of the story. The teacher leads the storytelling and invites individuals to supply words, sound effects, phrases or whole sentences. This way the detail is provided by the children while the development of the plot is controlled by the teacher.

Conscience alley or thought tunnel

This invites children to examine a moment in the drama in detail. It is employed most effectively when a decision has to be made, or when a decision has already been irrevocably made. Sometimes it requires the children to offer advice to a character, too. Children consider what they or the character might think about the decision and its implications.

The children stand in two lines facing each other about a metre apart. The teacher walks very slowly from one end of the 'alley' or tunnel to the other. As she does so, she turns to the child to one side and then to the other. They speak aloud a word or line (e.g. to Goldilocks, *You should leave this cottage*).

The thought tunnel offers a way of speaking a character's thoughts, rather than offering advice. The character moves through the tunnel in exactly the same way (e.g. as Goldilocks, *I should leave this cottage*).

Alleys or tunnels can be curved to represent the context, such as a winding path, and straight to represent the corridor leading to an important room. However, straight lines enable children to see and hear each other better.

Costuming

Selected props or items of clothing are chosen by the teacher to indicate a particular role to a class. It is important that any costume is put on in front of the children so they observe the teacher going into role in front of them. This ensures that there is no confusion about who the teacher actually is. Sometimes, with younger children, you can let them help you to put on items of clothing, helping with fastenings and giving advice as to which way around they go or which item to put in first. In many dramas the items are not immediately visible, so that the children bring them out of a bag or box one by one, guessing who might own such items.

Defining space

This is the way in which the teacher and class agree on the parameters and features of the fictional space. In the process the classroom space is defined as the place in the drama. It might be agreed that when we are facing the window side of the classroom we are facing the sea and the other side is inland. Items of furniture might be used to define the space. Two chairs, for example, might be used to define the gateposts leading to the castle. Children enjoy being part of the decision-making process and this enhances their commitment.

Discussion in role

Here the teacher and the children are in role discussing an issue or problem inside the drama. The conversation is not *about* the characters (e.g. *What do you think frightens him?*) but *between* the characters (e.g. *Do you understand why I am frightened?*). The discussion takes place *as if* the teacher and children are other people in another place; in a fictional context. Discussion in role may be set up as a formal meeting held to sort out problems or discuss plans. See **Meetings**.

Dramatic construction

We have used this term to describe moments when the children physically 'become' something inanimate – a bridge, a forest or a castle wall. It may be used to set the scene for action or to introduce an objective view on action. The forest trees, for example, can warn a deer that she is being followed or encourage her to run faster.

Dramatic play

Here children are indulging in imaginative play, but in the context of the shared drama. They may be preparing some food, making a toy or painting a rocket. The action is not controlled by the teacher, but the teacher may wander around among the children asking them about what they are doing as though she, too, is involved in the fiction: *What flavour is your cake going to be? How will you make that? How did you reach to paint that top bit?*

The children have freedom for individual creativity and are involved in their own worlds, so that one is baking a cake in a kitchen while another is shopping for drinks. High levels of concentration or emotion are not necessary in dramatic play, though of course they may occur. The activity helps to build up belief in the fiction. It is particularly useful with younger children.

Freeze frames/frozen pictures/still images/tableaux

We do not distinguish between these terms in this book. To make *freeze frames*, children arrange themselves as though they are in a three-dimensional picture, depicting a scene or a particular moment. It creates a frozen moment when we imagine time has stopped, giving us the opportunity to look at it more closely.

Freeze frames may be created by small groups, or by the whole group when they are often referred to as Collective still images or Collective Frozen pictures. They may be created quickly in the count to five, or they may be built one person at a time. This slower image-building approach enables children to respond to what others are doing in the image by placing themselves in a position that relates to another's. A child seeing someone else in an image on a swing in a park may stand behind the swing as though he is pushing it higher. Figures in freeze frames can be tapped on the shoulder and asked questions or their thoughts about something or someone in the drama. Freeze frames can be brought to life so they move into dramatic play and then frozen again with a clap of the hands. They can be reformed to show the future or the past. Captions can be voiced or written for freeze frames giving titles or moods. They are very flexible and are used often in these dramas in different ways.

Hot seating

Here one person in role as a character is asked questions by the rest of the class. The teacher is usually the best person to have in a hot seat since the pressure can be high and it involves thinking quickly. Also, the hot seat is often used to provide information, so the teacher is the one who can do this. It is a great way of teaching information. An example might be the teacher on the hot seat in role as a hospital doctor being asked about the function of the major organs in the body. The children do not have the information and the teacher wants them to ask questions in order to learn. Hence, it is helpful as a way to give information to children without being 'the teacher'. The children can ask questions directly to the character in the hot seat to find out whatever they wish to know. This requires them to think of the most appropriate questions and sometimes the best way of asking them. Sometimes there may be fictional pressure on them in the drama to find out all they can – if you don't know how the body works, you will not get through the interview for a job in the new class hospital. This heightens their motive to find out and the teacher's science objectives are achieved. Children may ask as themselves or in role as others in the drama.

Improvisation

The children act and speak in role. There is no pre-planning. Improvisation is often led by the teacher in role enabling her to keep control of the direction of the improvisation. All involved are speaking as characters in the drama.

Interviewing

Quite simply, the children and perhaps teacher are engaged in interviewing each other in role. Sometimes this can be carried out with children in pairs of A and B. They can take it in turns of being the interviewer. The roles of interviewers may be helpers who wish to understand someone or a situation better, or could be press or television journalists. Those being interviewed will be characters from the drama.

Meetings

This highly structured activity engages the teacher and children together in role, gathered for a specific purpose. This may be to hear new information, make plans or discuss strategies. The teacher will usually be the chair or leader at the meeting so that he can order the proceedings and ensure all the children's views are heard. Formal meetings are enhanced by an arrangement of chairs or benches in appropriate rows, and perhaps an agreed action when the Chair enters the room. Decisions about pace and procedures will depend upon the context of the meeting.

Narration and narration with mimed action

Teacher narration in drama activities is a useful strategy for setting the scene or moving the action along. It is often a very useful controlling device! The teacher is empowered to dictate particular aspects of the drama. A class working noisily, for example, may hear the teacher narrate, '*Gradually, they fell silent. The helpers were too tired to speak.*' Narration is also used to excite interest and build tension in the drama (e.g. *No one knew what was inside the bag. Some wondered if it might contain secrets while others felt sure it contained the lost treasure*). It may be used to set the scene (e.g. *The hall was enormous and richly decorated*) or to move the action forward (e.g. *They all packed their bags and started out on the dangerous journey*).

We enjoy drawing the children into narration through mimed action. *The villagers had to climb up over high rocks on their journey*, for example, would be accompanied by everyone miming climbing over imaginary rocks. It may also be used to help the children to imagine they are all one character (e.g. *She put on her big strong boots, tying the laces tightly. She then put on a heavy coat and did up the buttons, one, two, three and four*). Each child, in his or her own space, will mime the actions as the teacher narrates.

The opportunities for engaging children in the narration are described under **Storytelling** below.

Overheard conversations

Children in groups make up conversations that people in their drama may have had. They then overhear one another's conversations as though they are eavesdropping. This enables the children to work in small groups and gives all of them the chance to comment in role on the action of the drama. The easiest way to set this up is for the groups to have time improvising first, before being asked to fall silent. You then wander around the room stopping to eavesdrop on the groups in turn. In this way, all the children are actually eavesdropping since they are all quiet. They are also waiting for the moment when you stand near them and they must have their conversation. As you walk away from them they fade out and the group you approach start their conversation. It is fun if you move away in mid-sentence to create some suspense. When you return to the group they will pick up where they left off and more is revealed to the class.

Ritual

Ritual is a repeated procedure that those in the drama are familiar with and value highly. In drama a ritual is used to give action significance. Any action, no matter how mundane, may be performed in a formal and dignified manner to make the actions seem to matter. Putting items into a picnic basket, for example, by having one child at a time step forward to place an imaginary contribution into the basket announcing what it is, brings about a more serious level of thought to the action and a more exciting atmosphere. While not a ritual in the strictest sense, it creates attention and status to the action.

Role on the wall

The outline of a character in the drama is drawn on to a large sheet of paper. This could even be a stick figure if you are not very confident drawing. Information about the character in the drama is collected and written around the outline. It is possible to contrast different types of information in a role on the wall. What the character says can be written in one colour and what she thinks in another. Sometimes the character's thoughts are written in the round head of the role on the wall and what other people think about the character is written around the outside of the figure.

Sculpting

This way of working involves children making statues of each other or the teacher through suggestions and/or physical manipulation. Sculptures can be made to crystallize ideas about a character, such as what the bully looked like; or to express a feeling, such as how anger could be physically represented. Children might suggest that the bully holds her head higher or has a hand on the waist. Sculpting enables different ideas to be seen represented. The class may wish to agree one particular stance at the end of their exploration.

Sound collage/soundscapes

Soundscapes are created by the children. This can be achieved in different ways. A sound collage may accompany a journey with sounds accompanying the group or teacher in role climbing a mountain or travelling through a forest at night. Children might represent the features of the forest, as a tree with rustling branches or an owl hooting. Sound collages are creative and provide an opportunity for those not so confident in speaking out loud to participate orally. The sounds can also be made using objects or musical instruments.

Statementing

Statementing involves the children in making statements about a person, event or place in the drama. The statements may be made in a ritualistic manner, with children stepping forward one at a time to give their statement. They may remain frozen in a gesture appropriate to the statement while others make their statements, or they may return to their original place and watch the others. It is a way of involving the children in the construction or consideration of events or characters so that they have a sense of ownership. It can be useful to slow the drama down with some serious thought, such as statements about what people would say about the girl who has just stolen a pencil case.

Still images/freeze frames/frozen pictures/tableaux

We do not distinguish between these terms in this book. See *freeze frames* for detailed description.

Storytelling

This activity includes different modes of storytelling. Sometimes the teacher provides narration with pauses that the children fill in, as described above under *Collaborative storytelling*. This involves them in the storytelling and makes their contribution part of the whole. At other times storytelling is suggested as a way to involve all the children in reviewing the events of the drama. Here each child takes it in turns to tell a line of the story, as in a story circle. Older children may divide into small groups to story tell the events of their drama together.

Teacher in role

The teacher takes the role of someone in the drama. This enables the teacher to work with the children from inside the drama. Additional information may be given through the teacher's role, as described in *Hot seating* above, for example. A teacher in role can pose questions to challenge the children's ideas and assumptions. Discipline can be maintained through the teacher in role, which is usually more effective and less disruptive than when we discipline as teachers. For example, if children are being noisy. Teacher in role explains that since the recent events she has suffered from terrible headaches and she won't be able to tell them where the treasure lies unless they speak quietly. Or, for example, the teddy bears mustn't wake up, so we will all have to whisper. Teacher in role is used in many approaches listed in this glossary, such as meetings, hot seating, whole-class improvisation and dramatic play.

Thought tracking and thought tapping

Thought tracking enables children in role to speak aloud the thoughts that would normally remain concealed. This can be done in different ways, such as **Conscience alleys** or **thought tunnels**, described above. The thoughts of characters could also be tracked during a mime. Another form of thought tracking might be created by placing an object or character in the centre of a circle of children who offer advice or thoughts.

Thought tapping is when the teacher literally taps a child on the shoulder as a signal for the child to speak the thoughts of the character he is playing. Thought tapping is also used in conjunction with mimed activity or most commonly with freeze frames. Once the children are doing either of these, the teacher moves among them and taps them on the shoulder one at a time. She may ask about what the children are doing, about what they are thinking or feeling, or about what they can see or smell or hear from where they are. It invites children to commit further to their roles and to the drama, and to think further about the context. Their contributions become part of the shared understanding of the imaginary place and people. It is a quite controlled activity that gives less vocal individuals their moment.

Whole-group improvisation

This activity involves the children and the teacher working together in role. The teacher will have teacher intentions in mind, but the ideas and suggestions offered by the children, and therefore the responses of the teacher will vary when working with different groups. It is this mode of activity which often generates a high level of concentration and emotional commitment. Unlike dramatic play, the children are all engaged in one world, dealing with the same problem.

Drama games

A cleared space is needed for all these games and a circle of chairs is required for 'Fruit salad'.

Captain's coming!

The teacher explains the commands that the children must respond to. They imagine they are on board a large ship/sailing vessel. '*Captain's coming!*' means that they all stand still with a straight back and a salute. '*Bombs overhead!*' means that they lie on the floor face down with arms and legs straight. '*Scrub the decks!*' means that they mime scrubbing the decks.

You can designate directions and include '*Port!*' and '*Starboard*'. You can use a few commands to begin with and build in more as the children get better at remembering and responding quickly.

The teacher or a child calls out the commands and the children get into the appropriate positions as quickly as possible. The last one into the correct position is out. The winner is the person left in at the end. Between commands, the children can move around the space not touching each other. You could play music such as a sea shanty and turn it down as you call the commands. If the children can dance the hornpipe they may do so between commands!

This is a fun, energetic activity. Children have to be ready to respond very quickly to instructions so it does require concentration. It encourages speedy reactions. You can adapt the game for different contexts. '*Teacher's coming!!*' in a school-based drama might generate commands such as '*Line up*' and '*Sit in a circle*'. The children can make up commands for the game.

Fruit salad

The children sit on chairs in a circle. There should be no empty chairs. Each child is allocated one of three names (e.g. apple, mango or banana). A caller stands in the middle of the circle and calls out one of the fruits (e.g. mango), and all the mangoes have to leave their seats and rush to find another chair to sit on. The caller's aim is to sit on a chair too. Whoever is left without a chair is the next caller. If 'Fruit salad' is called, everyone has to leave their chairs and find another. Players are not allowed to return to the chairs they have just vacated. When their fruit is called they must find new chairs. The aim for everybody is to ensure they are sitting on a chair.

This game can be adapted to introduce different vocabulary relevant to the context of the drama, such as ice-cream, beach hut and sandcastle in the drama 'Beside the seaside'. Any names, terms or even descriptive words may be used. This is a fun way to introduce new or difficult vocabulary to children. New words introduced in the game will soon become familiar.

Grandmother's footsteps

Person A faces a wall at one end of the room and the children all face her at the other end. A turns around at random intervals. The children's aim is to creep up behind A without being seen to move when A looks around. The first to reach A taps her shoulder and wins the game. A's aim is to make sure that no one achieves this. The winner can take A's place.

This game is about physical control, concentration and challenge. It creates a building up of tension as people get nearer to A. A similar game is 'What's the time, Mr Wolf?' This game could be used in 'Jack and the Beanstalk' in preparation for creeping up on the Giant. See p. 78.

Keeper of the keys

Person A sits blindfolded on a chair in the middle of the space. There is a bunch of keys or other jingling object beneath the chair. The others stand at some distance in a wide circle around the chair. Their aim is to get the keys. A's aim is to ensure that the keys remain under the chair.

Those around the edge must move as quietly as they can towards the chair. If A hears any sound, she points in the direction of the sound. Whoever is pointed at must move back to the perimeter of the circle and begin again. Whoever is able to grab the keys without being pointed at is the winner and takes the place of person A.

This can also be played with individuals approaching the chair one at a time.

This game involves physical control and coordination as well as concentration. It may be used with a different item under the chair that is relevant to the drama.

Chapter 1
The Sad Clown

The children meet a very miserable clown who is in need of their help. The clown has always wanted to work in the circus but is in danger of being thrown out because he can't make the audience laugh. The children teach the clown how to be funny.

Learning Objectives

- To give advice to help solve a problem;
- To sequence activities to make a successful routine for the clown.

Themes

- Helping others
- Having fun
- Identifying aspects of performance.

Resources

- Books about or pictures of the circus;
- Suggested props and/or costume for clown – red nose, hat, juggling balls or oranges, large hanky.
- Optional face paints.
- A full clown costume is a bonus;
- Oversized and colourful bag containing any props.

Time

- This session can take between thirty minutes and an hour.

Notes

The drama can be taught with no resources at all. However, they add to the 'theatre' of the experience. This is potentially a fairly physical drama session for the teacher, depending on which tricks the children suggest that you do. It may be worth laying down some ground rules when you first go in to role as the clown, saying that you have a bad back that will prevent you from doing anything too adventurous. Otherwise, be prepared to do forward rolls and stand on your head – the children always think this is very funny!

What do we know about the circus?

Teacher's intentions

● To activate the children's prior knowledge and understanding about the circus

Questioning and discussion: sharing information and introducing the story

Introduce the drama by leading a general discussion about circuses. This may need to be done using a picture or even a storybook with which the children may be familiar.

● *Has anyone ever been* with *to a circus or seen one on television?*
● *What happens at the circus?*
● *What kinds of acts could you see?*
● *Who is in charge at the circus?*
● *What does the ringmaster usually wear to look smart and important?*
● *What do the clowns do?*
● *Do clowns wear any special clothes?*

Tell the children that they are going to tell a story about a circus in their drama today. Tell them that there is going to be a special person in the story that they are going to meet. If you are using a bag of props, the children are told that this person is the owner of the bag.

 Discussion, including relevant detail – choose specific vocabulary

Read a storybook about the circus, e.g. *Spot Goes to the Circus* by Eric Hill

Optional activity: What is in the bag? Looking at the clown's costume and teacher dressing as the clown

Teacher's intentions

● To use the items of clothing to build up a picture of the clown

Opening the bag: discussion of the clothing/props

Place the bag of clothes or clown props in the centre of the circle of children. Invite children one at a time to take something out of the bag. Ask the child to describe what he or she has found. Encourage children to comment on each item:

● *What do you think this is?*
● *What kind of person would need/wear this?*
● *What do you think the balls/oranges are for?*
● *This is a strange hat! Who would wear one like this?*

Lay the items out on the floor for everyone to see.

 Prediction, description, focus on relevant detail

Costuming: teacher putting on the costume

Tell the children that in the story you are going to be the clown who owns these things and that you are going to wear the costume or have these things (hat, juggling balls and red nose). You may need help with dressing or deciding how to hold things correctly, so you could invite the children to help you dress. Alternatively, they can suggest the order for putting on the clothes. As you are being dressed, it is important to keep up a commentary about what is happening, and you can ask more questions to gather the children's collective knowledge about clowns and circuses. If you are feeling confident or are working with a small group of children, you may invite them to paint your face to make you look like a clown.

- *Has anyone ever seen a clown?*
- *What do clowns do?*
- *How do they make people laugh?*
- *Is this a man or a lady clown?*
- *What do you think is a good name for a clown?*

Take a few suggestions of names and choose one for the clown who the children are going to meet.

Now that you are dressed as the clown, or are holding the clown's props, tell the children that they are going to be able to speak to the clown in a couple of minutes. How do they expect the clown to behave? Will he or she be happy? Jumping about? Tell the children that the clown will come and talk to them now. Walk away from the children and return in role as the clown.

 Description – include relevant detail, ask questions to clarify understanding

Draw clown faces and write chosen names underneath

Find out information about famous clowns. Collect pictures from websites.
Use words to describe the clowns

Figure 1.1 Sad clown by Phoebe

Meeting the sad clown

Teacher's intentions

- To introduce the teacher in role
- To encourage children to offer advice
- For children to use an appropriate tone and register

Teacher in role: meeting the clown and giving advice

The teacher, in role as the clown, enters, with a very sad face, pulls out a large hanky, blows nose loudly and sighs. *Oh dear, whatever shall I do? I'm so miserable.*

Hopefully the children will ask what is wrong. If they don't (which is very unlikely), you could add: *No one seems to care about me*, and if necessary: *I suppose you are not interested in me either, are you?*

The clown tells the children his or her story: *I've wanted to be a clown all my life. I used to go to the circus and laugh at the clowns and wish that I could be one. Then the other day I was walking past this circus tent when the ringmaster ran out asking if anyone could help him. The clown had got the chicken pox and couldn't go on that night. I knew that was my chance to be a clown and I told the ringmaster that I could do it. So, he gave me a job! But I wasn't any good at all. No one laughed at me. The ringmaster said I was useless and if I wasn't any better tonight then I would have to leave. I don't want to leave. I love working here. I didn't think that I was too bad, really. What can I do?*

The children will probably ask you what things you did, but if not you can ask them: *Shall I show you what I did?* Then give an example of a pathetic joke with a slow delivery, a miserable face and a useless attempt at acrobatics or juggling! Some children may laugh at this anyway, but in role you need to say that the ringmaster was not pleased at all.

Ask the children to suggest how the clown's act can be improved and suggest some exciting things to put into the show tonight.

Invite individual children to demonstrate suggestions and try to copy them, badly at first, then improving. Suggestions should come freely from the children, but a few possibilities may include:

- Introducing the show in a loud voice
- Big gestures
- Telling funny jokes with a smile
- Falling over or rolling
- Juggling with the balls or oranges (you don't have to be successful, but assure the children you will practise)
- Throwing buckets of pretend water
- Funny walks
- Balancing on one leg and toppling over in a hilarious way.

As the children make more suggestions and you try things out you can grow in confidence. The whole group can be encouraged to stand up and join in with 'practising' the stunts.

- *Do you think I'm getting better?*
- *Should I do it like this or would it look better like this?*
- *How should my face look?*
- *Would it be a good idea to make these things into a little show?*
- *Perhaps we could write a list of the things that I am going to do in the right order so I don't forget.*

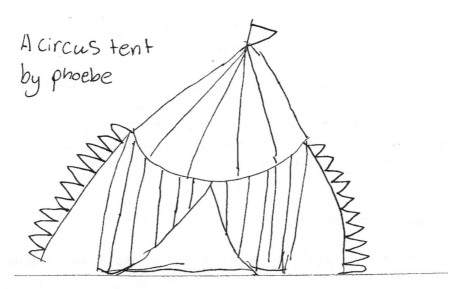

Figure 1.2 A circus tent by Phoebe

Listening and responding, making relevant comments, taking account of different people and adapting what they say, speaking to different people

Giving reasons for opinions

Creating speech bubbles for the clown and the ringmaster

Writing a list of the clown's routine

Making a list and rehearsing the show

Teacher's intentions

● For children to help to sequence the routine.

Demonstration and rehearsal: practising the show

The clown asks the children to decide in which order to perform the stunts. The order can be written down or remembered, whichever is appropriate. Perform the show in the right order, asking the children to prompt you. Usually there is spontaneous applause! Ask the children to suggest if there are any improvements. Take their advice. Tell the children it is time for your show now and thank them for their help. Leave waving merrily and take off the costume.

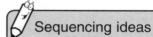 Sequencing ideas

Storyboarding the routine. Ask the children to draw a series of pictures to illustrate the clown's routine with the main verb written below, for example: juggling

Narration/storytelling: how did the story end?

Finish the story by asking the children what they think happened that night. Use their ideas to narrate a satisfactory ending such as:

The clown was an enormous success that night. The ringmaster couldn't believe his eyes. The crowd laughed and clapped so loudly you could hear the noise miles away. The ringmaster thanked the clown for a splendid performance and offered him a permanent job in the circus. The clown worked happily there for many years and always remembered the day that his friends, the children, showed him how to be a very funny clown.

Reflection: what have we learned?

Discuss the story. Was the clown as the children had expected? How had they helped the clown?

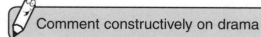 Comment constructively on drama

Writing – the clown's story

Composing newspaper headlines

Writing a programme entry for the new clown

Designing a poster advertising the circus

Chapter 2
The Teddy Bears' Picnic

It doesn't seem to be a very good day for the teddy minder. The teddies, now asleep in a basket, hadn't wanted to have their afternoon nap, so she had promised that when they awoke she would take them on a teddy bears' picnic. The trouble is that she isn't sure what you do on a teddy bears' picnic. The children offer her advice about the games to play and songs to sing. They make a picnic of all the things they think the teddies will like to eat and drink. They then join the picnic and look after the teddies until they are tired and ready for bed.

They need to speak quietly, so as not to wake the sleeping teddies: this means that all the children whisper. This is a useful control during discussion, because only one person can be heard at a time. The teacher in role can sometimes appear excited by a child's idea and exclaim loudly and then, putting a hand over her mouth, indicate that she has stupidly forgotten that she must keep quiet.

Learning objectives

- To help children learn the significance of ordering instructions;
- To encourage a sense of responsibility for others;
- To give children an experience of helping an adult;
- To develop vocabulary.

Themes

- Helping others
- Food
- Giving advice.

Resources

- A large container or a basket – a plastic washing basket is ideal;
- A tea-cloth to cover the teddies in the basket;
- As many teddies/soft toys as there are children in the group – or enough for them to share;
- *Optional*: paper cut into shapes of food that children can colour in (e.g. banana, burger in a bun, orange, honey jar);
- *Optional*: props for a shop and a kitchen;
- *Optional*: paper cut into teddy bear shapes to be decorated/coloured in.

Ideally, the words to the song are presented on screen.

Time

- One hour.

Notes

When the teddy bears are given out to the children, there is the chance to create specific individual traits in the bears that may be appropriate for particular children. Perhaps a child who can get a little over-excited could be given a bear who easily gets anxious. *He's a fun bear, but needs to feel cared for.* A child with low self-esteem and status with peers might be apparently pointed out by the biggest bear in the basket. *Did you say you have seen someone who you would like to be with?*, Teddy is whispering in your ear. *All the children here are nice children. Pardon? There is someone special for you, is there? Would you like to point out who you mean?* Move the bear's arm to indicate the child. It gives the child an ego boost and presents him with a positive – indeed, enviable – image in front of the other children.

Figure 2.1 The Teddy Bears' Picnic by Charlie

THE TEDDY BEARS' PICNIC

If you go down in the woods today
You're sure of a big surprise.
If you go down in the woods today
You'd better go in disguise.
For every bear that ever there was
Will gather there for certain, because
Today's the day the teddy bears have their picnic.

Every teddy bear who's been good
Is sure of a treat today.
There's lots of marvellous things to eat
And wonderful games to play.
Beneath the trees, where nobody sees,
They'll hide and seek as long as they please.
'Cos that's the way the teddy bears have their picnic.

If you go down in the woods today
You'd better not go alone.
It's lovely down in the woods today
But safer to stay at home.
For every bear that ever there was
Will gather there for certain, because
Today's the day the teddy bears have their picnic.

Picnic time for teddy bears,
The little teddy bears are having a lovely time today.
Watch them, catch them unawares,
And see them picnic on their holiday.
See them gaily gather 'bout,
They love to play and shout
They never have any cares.
At six o'clock their mummies and daddies
Will take them home to bed
Because they're tired little teddy bears.

Lyrics by Jimmy Kennedy.

Meeting the teddy minder

Teacher's intentions

- To introduce the problem to be solved;
- To give children the experience of being the experts;
- To develop sensitive communication and volume control.

Teacher in role: setting the scene

Enter the space carefully carrying the basket. It is full of teddy bears concealed by the tea-cloth laid over the top. Very carefully, and with great concentration, place it in the centre of the circle. Whisper:

Ssshh. All the teddies are having a sleep. Poor little things. They were so excited about this and now they are going to be so sad when they wake up and find out. I feel very upset about it.

The children may ask what is wrong at this point.

The teddy bears had not wanted to go to sleep, so I stupidly said that if they settled down for their after-lunch sleep, I would take them for a teddy bears' picnic. The trouble is that I don't know what teddy bears do at a teddy bears' picnic. Oh dear. They will be so upset.

Attentive listening and responses

Discussion in role: children advise

The children will often offer advice themselves, but if not, they can be asked if they can help or if they know anything about teddy bears' picnics.

- *What do they play?*
- *Where do they go for the picnic?*
- *What do they eat?*
- *Isn't there a special song? Something about going down in the woods today ...?*

It is important that the teacher in role continues asking questions as the children explain, encouraging them to clarify their explanations and ordering the explanations appropriately.

- *Sandwiches! But I don't know what to put inside the sandwiches. What might they like?*
- *How do you play hide-and-seek?*
- *For how long does the person shut his eyes?*
- *If I am hiding, how do I know when you are coming to look for me?*
- *But what goes after 'Ring a Ring of Roses'?*
- *Oh, that sounds wonderful! Will you teach me the song?*

Sequencing

Descriptions

Listen to the song following the lines on screen, and/or sing the song while pointing to the words

Instructions: created a set of instructions together for playing a game

Play party games, such as Ring a Ring of Roses

Read other rhymes and stories about teddies

Picnic preparations

Teacher's intentions

- To encourage use of imagination;
- To invite children to bring their own tastes and experiences into the pretend context;
- To practise talking to different people.

Dramatic play: preparing the picnic

Ask the children if they would help prepare the picnic and invite them to come too.

Shall we make the picnic first? We should all get something for the picnic and meet here when the clock strikes three. I will have a picnic basket here ready.

(Move the teddies to 'somewhere quiet' where the children will not be tempted to touch them.)

Some children like to pretend to make sandwiches through mimed activity, others to go to a pretend shop to buy bottled drinks. Move about the space from being in the kitchen, asking one child about the cooking processes to being the shopkeeper who sells bananas to another. The space may be organized so that one end is where the shop is and the other is the kitchen. This may be done with or without any concrete props, such as scales and cookers.

If there is an imaginary play area set up as a kitchen, it is used here.

Imagining and creating roles and using appropriate words

Interacting with others to get things done

Children draw pictures of the food they have prepared, or they colour in prepared shapes, and describe their food item

Following instructions for making fruit jellies or sandwiches

Ritual: packing the picnic

Indicate the clock striking three, saying 'Dong' loudly or using an instrument. The children are asked to sit in a circle. The teacher moves into the circle and mimes opening a huge bag, explaining as she does so:

- *This is a very special bag. It can hold as much as we want to put in it.*

The children watch as the teacher moves back to the edge of the circle, picks up an imaginary cake, carries it to the centre and places it in the bag with care. As she does so, she announces, for example,

- *A large creamy chocolate cake with chocolate drops on top.*

Children take it in turns around the circle to pick up the food or drink that they have brought and place it in the bag, announcing what it is. Teacher may ask questions about some of them:

- *How will they eat the jelly?*
- *What flavour are the crisps?*
- *Why did you choose honey for the sandwiches?*

Or provide comments as a way of supporting the child's choice:

- *Ooh! I adore raspberry jam!*
- *Thank goodness you remembered drinks! I had forgotten!*
- *I have heard that teddies love oranges!*

 Speaking aloud and responding to questions

Listening to music/singing: listen to a recording of the song 'The Teddy Bears' Picnic'

Preparations

Teacher's intentions

- To encourage an understanding of the need for organization and planning;
- To introduce the teddies in a sympathetic light to encourage a caring response.

Discussion in role

Explain that before the teddies wake up you want to be clear about what will happen.

- *What do we do first? Eat or sing or play games?*
- *Which game, then?*

The children agree the order of events and it is reiterated so that the minder understands. She may need prompting.

- *So, it's hide-and-seek and then ... Sorry, which game do we do next?*
- *Oh dear, I am glad that you will be with me because I can't remember when we have the food.*

The children are asked if they would be prepared to look after a teddy each (or in twos or threes).

- *I know that I am asking you to do a very grown-up job and that you will have to be very gentle with the teddies, but I would be so grateful for your help.*

 Ordering and clarifying information

Whole-group improvisation: being teddy minders

Carefully bring the basket to the circle. Peep under the tea-cloth and whisper that the bears seem to be waking. Very gently and slowly lift the tea-cloth off, which will reveal the teddies and soft toys to the children for the first time.

Select one teddy and gently lift it out of the basket, perhaps telling the children its name and something about it.

Now, Andrew Bear is very friendly, but I need someone to look after him who will keep an eye on him when he is having his picnic. He does tend to spill his food down his front. Here is Woolly. He will sing all day if he can. Who will enjoy singing our special song with Woolly?

Each teddy is given to a child. The teacher must handle the bears very gently to provide a positive role model of a teddy minder. Each child will usually handle the teddy according to how it is given.

The Teddy Bears' Picnic

Teacher's intentions

- To develop responsibility for others (albeit teddies in this context);
- To participate in the planned event;
- To put the teddies to bed to complete the cycle of their day.

Dramatic play: the party

The plans are carried out as organized by the children. For circle games, each teddy will be between two children, so they will hold the bears' paws.

- *Who will tell the bears what we have planned for them next?*
- *You may need to sing more loudly to help them remember the words.*

The children and bears are asked to sit down for the picnic. Children might be given napkins to use for the bears, or wet wipes could be passed around. They will need to wash/wipe the teddies' paws both before and after their food!

Ritual: putting the teddies to bed

After the activities have been carried out, everyone sits in a circle with the children holding the bears.

It has been such a lovely day. Thank you so much for your help. I couldn't have done any of this without all of you. I know the teddies have had a wonderful time. It's time for them to go to bed now after their busy afternoon. Could you say goodnight to them and then I shall call each of you in turn to put your teddy back into the basket.

One by one the teddies are put into the basket again and finally the tea-cloth is placed over the top 'so they can sleep'.

The children select a lullaby to sing to send the teddies off to sleep.

Storytelling: children explain about what they did with their bear at the picnic. They might include what it ate, whether it was a messy eater, had washed its hands and which games it had most enjoyed

Children bring their favourite teddies to school and use adjectives to describe them

Reflection: what have we learned?

- Discuss the events
- How did the children help?

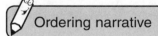

Ordering narrative

Teacher shows pictures of teddy bears, and the children say which ones they like and why

Re-tell the story chronologically

Chapter 3
The Not-So-Jolly Postman

The children find that the postman, normally a happy, easygoing person, is very sad. He is embarrassed to explain that he is frightened of a dog in the front garden of a house on his round. Ms Woof, who is new in the village, does not understand why anyone could be frightened of her dog and has to be convinced that there is a problem. The children negotiate a resolution. But all this takes time, and now the postman is afraid that he won't get all the letters delivered on time. The children learn about the addresses and help him by delivering the letters themselves through the horizontal and vertical letterboxes.

Learning objectives

- To develop number recognition;
- To encourage reading for a purpose;
- To consider others and their fears;
- To invite negotiation and problem-solving.

Themes

- Post delivery
- Using tact and negotiation
- Problem-solving.

Resources

- Drawings of doors on large sheets of sugar paper;
- A bag suitable to use as a postal worker's bag;
- Addressed envelopes are required. Children may make these or they can be prepared by the teacher earlier;
- Addresses displayed on a board for all to read.

Time

- One hour and thirty minutes.

Notes

You may wish to use local names so that children become familiar with their shapes and sounds. It is useful to have some familiar words for the names, to enhance recognition and perhaps spelling.

Table 3.1

Ms C. Woof 1 Happy Lane Sunlea Northamptonshire	Mrs J. Wig and Mr E. Ogun Lane End Cottage Sunlea Northamptonshire	Mr R. and Mrs T. Jolly 3 Happy Lane Sunlea Northamptonshire
Miss S. Singh Sun Farm Sunlea Northamptonshire	Doctor Pill 2 Happy Lane Sunlea Northamptonshire	Miss O'Casey 4 Happy Lane Sunlea Northamptonshire

Doors are drawn by the teacher on large sheets of sugar paper in preparation. They should all be slightly different, with either a vertical or horizontal letterbox flap cut into them. Each should also have a number from 1 to 4 or a house name, either 'Sun Farm' or 'Lane End Cottage'. The doors can be very simple or more elaborate.

Figure 3.1 Doors

The postman's problem

Teacher's intentions

- To use supportive language
- To resolve a problem
- To practise negotiation skills.

Discussion: why is the postman sad?

The postman was usually a very jolly postman, but this morning he is not very jolly at all. In fact, he is very sad and hasn't left for his delivery. Why might he be sad?

Predictions are made and ideas are discussed. Invite the children to meet the postman to see if they can find out from him why he is so sad. They can plan how they might cheer him up and what sorts of questions they might ask him. Place a chair where they can all see it.

The teacher explains that when she is on the chair, she will be the postman.

Teacher in role: meeting the postman

The postman looks very glum, twisting the strap of the bag anxiously and looking down. If the children don't speak to him, he may look up and say, *Hello. I am sorry not to be more welcoming to you.*

He doesn't offer much more, but gradually responds to the children's question giving the information about his problem:

I love my job, but I can't do it anymore ... It is too embarrassing to talk about ... You will think that I am silly ...

Someone new has moved into the village ... I can't deliver there ...

My friend got bitten by a tiny dog in the next village ... and this new dog is huge. It is always in the front garden.

The children offer to help. The postman has his doubts. Usually, the children will wish to go to see Ms Woof, the dog owner.

But what will you say? Why should she take any notice?

The postman does not want to go with them since he is embarrassed (and because the teacher will take the role of Ms Woof!).

 Attentive listening and response

 Write a list of words that mean 'happy' and a list that mean 'sad'

Practise making happy and sad faces. Read the words aloud in random order. The children make the appropriate expression to check that they remember what all the words mean

Read stories about postal workers, such as *The Jolly Postman* books by Janet and Allan Ahlberg and *Postman Pat* books by John Cuncliffe.

Whole-group improvisation: meeting Ms Woof

Agree on where the front gate into Ms Woof's garden is and use a chair to indicate the front of the house. Ms Woof will be washing up by the front window. The children agree among themselves who will speak first and how they will attract Ms Woof's attention. The children will explain the problem as Ms Woof mimes holding a huge dog that may jerk her arm forward from time to time!

Ms Woof responds

You must be mistaken. No one could be afraid of Giant/Rover/Warrior [choose a name that implies it's a big tough dog]. *Maybe the postman is being silly ... our last postman loved him! He is causing trouble without knowing the dog ...*

The children will argue the postman's case and Ms Woof can argue on every front. Eventually some solution will need to be reached (e.g. the postman meets the dog, brings it treats, it is tied up for the first few weeks or even in the house or back garden). Flushed with success, they go to tell the postman. (This could end the drama, or lead to the next stage.)

 Finding the right things to say in a difficult context

 Sign-making: make signs to say 'Beware of the Dog'. These could be illustrated

Discussion about how dogs are trained. Who has dogs? What have they been trained to do?

Delivering the letters

Teacher's intentions

- To develop number identification
- To encourage reading skills
- To match words and/or letters.

Preparing the letters: can we deliver them?

Envelopes need to be prepared if they have not been pre-prepared. A few names and addresses are displayed and each child is given an envelope. Some children may copy the addresses while others may be given an envelope with part of it already written and they match the rest. All the envelopes are put into the postbag.

 Matching, reading and writing

Teacher in role: the postman is persuaded

The postman is concerned that he has no time to deliver the letters now that he has wasted so much time over worrying about the dog.

● *I will get into such trouble if the letters are not delivered on time ... there is no way I will get them done now.*

Children are always desperate to deliver the letters, but the postman needs to be persuaded.

● *You won't know where all the houses are ...*
● *I know about the different letterboxes ...*
● *You may put envelopes in the wrong door.*

In the end he is persuaded and shows the children the addresses on a board. They repeat the words in the addresses as he points to them. Some will soon be familiar, since they are written on the envelopes. When the postman feels confident that the children are ready to deliver the letters to the right doors, he waves them goodbye, asking them to be very careful.

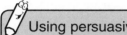 Using persuasive language

Dramatic play: delivering the letters

The teacher gets out the sugar paper doors and pins/sticks the top corners on to the tops of tables around the room, explaining that they will imagine the classroom is the village. The postman opens his bag and passes each child one letter at a time.

The children find the appropriate door to post their envelope into. Some children like to retrieve their letters for the experience of doing it again and look at all the doors again as though for the first time.

Describe your front door. What colour is it? Is there a doorknob? Are there any windows in the door? Who has horizontal or vertical letter boxes?

Figure 3.2 Using front doors

Whole-class improvisation: updating the postman

Once all the letters are delivered, the postman invites the children to come for a drink and cake to show his appreciation. As he mimes passing cake around, the children are invited to describe their delivery. Had they seen any dogs? Were any letterboxes awkward? Did they see any friends on their way?

 Using descriptive language and sequencing

Children tell of their letter deliveries as a story

Reflection: what have we learned?

- Review what has happened in the drama;
- Reflect on the children's achievements;
- Consider how the drama may impact on their lives outside the classroom;
- What were the postman's problems?
- Do the children know anyone who is afraid of dogs or other animals?
- How will things be different for the postman at Ms Woof's house?
- How did the children bring this about?
- Are there other things that can be sorted out by talking and listening?

Writing letters – this could include emergent letter writing

ICT – use the programmable floor robots to deliver letters to different houses on a map

Chapter 4
The Baker's Shop

Mr Baker is a much-loved and respected figure in the village, well known for his delicious bread and cakes. One day the children are disturbed to find that his shop window is empty. What could be the problem? The children are invited to help the incapacitated baker make bread and cakes. They are also asked to help design and make a surprise birthday cake for the King. When they deliver the cake to the palace they find that the King has toothache because he has failed to take care of his teeth. The children teach him how to brush his teeth properly and make regular visits to the 'Tendist'.

Learning objectives

- To be able to help and give advice;
- To understand the importance of dental hygiene.

Resources

- Felt pens, large picture of shop front (see Figure 4.1)
- Optional props for baker: apron, wooden spoon
- Letter from the Queen (see Figures 4.2 and 4.3)
- Optional props for the King: cloak, crown.

Time

- Minimum of one hour.

Let's talk about bakeries

Teacher's intentions

- To focus thinking on bakeries and bakers;
- To activate and collect knowledge and understanding.

Discussion: what do we know about bakers?

Introduce the session by leading a general discussion about bakers' shops.

We're going to tell a story today and it's going to be about a baker's shop. Has anyone ever been to a baker's shop? Does anyone know the name of the shop where you buy bread? Supermarkets do sell bread, you're quite right, but can you think of a special little shop?

This may be difficult for some children, but you can introduce the idea of the baker's shop and the baker who makes the bread and cakes, if necessary.

What else do you buy in the shop?
What is your favourite bread/cake/biscuit?

Encourage children to say why they like particular products.

> Choosing appropriate vocabulary, listening to others' ideas

Narration and collective drawing: the baker's shop window

Introduce the idea that the drama today is going to be about a baker's shop that is in a small village. Show the children a picture of it, using a pre-prepared shop front outline on paper or on the whiteboard (see Figure 4.1). Introduce the fact that strangely enough this baker's shop is owned by Mr Baker! Mr Baker has owned the shop and baked bread and cakes there for as long as anyone can remember. Everyone knows him. He is friendly and well liked.

Children are invited to draw pictures of their favourite cake, bread or biscuit into the outline of the window.

Keep the dialogue going while the children are coming one or two at a time to draw their pictures:

Figure 4.1 The Baker's Shop

- *What have you chosen as your favourite?*
- *What colour is the icing?*
- *Has the bun got cherries on the top?*
- *What does it taste like?*
- *What does it smell like?*

Alternatively, children can be given post-it notes to draw bread and cakes on. These can then be stuck on to the shop window. This saves time and is easier to organise.

Label the cakes in Mr Baker's window

Write a description of your favourite cake/sandwich/bread

Collect pictures and find out the names of different types of bread. These could be from different countries

Some cakes/bread/biscuits by Phoebe

Figure 4.2 Some cakes/bread/biscuits by Phoebe

Narration: introducing the problem of the empty shop window

Use the completed picture of the shop window as you continue to narrate the story:

Every morning the children stop to look in the window at the cakes on their way to school. He was well known for making the best [ask children to say which cakes they have drawn] *in the whole world. Mr Baker often makes extra biscuits for them to put in their lunchboxes for snacks.*

   One morning, the children looked in the window and it was ... empty!

Discussion: what has happened to Mr Baker?

Ask the children to suggest possible reasons for the empty window, (for example, burglary, Mr Baker is ill, or he's still asleep). Accept all of these suggestions as possibilities and say that any of them could have happened.

 Make suggestions, discuss options, give reasons

Use thought bubbles to record ideas about what might have happened

Meeting Mr Baker

Teacher's intentions

- To introduce the teacher in role;
- For children to take on roles in the drama and build belief in the story.

Planning roles, defining space and introducing teacher in role

Tell the children that they are going to be the children in the story and that they will be able to find out what has happened to Mr Baker. Set up the space together by deciding where the door of the shop will be and where they are going to stand to look through the window. Decide who will knock on the door and whether they will shout through the letterbox. Tell the children that in the next part of the story you are going to be Mr Baker and that you will wait in a certain place until you hear them call out a given phrase. You may decide to wear an apron or carry a wooden spoon to indicate when you are in role.

Teacher in role as Mr Baker hobbles to the door clutching his back and muttering:

Oh dear me. I wonder who this can be. Oh dear. Ouch. I'm coming ... (He painfully unbolts the door and smiles weakly at the children) ... Hello everyone. How nice to see you. Oh dear.

Hopefully, someone will ask what the matter is and why the shop isn't open today. Mr Baker explains that he has a bad back. He strained it lifting a bag of flour yesterday. The doctor has told him to rest for a few days. The problem is that he has no one to help him so he won't be able to cook anything or open the shop for a while. Usually the children offer to lend a hand, but Mr Baker will need to be persuaded that they know something about cooking before he agrees to their kind offer. Ask them about any previous cooking they have done at home. Do they know what 'ingredients' are? Do they know what goes in the middle of doughnuts or on the top of birthday cakes?

 Listen to others, ask and answer questions, give reasons for opinions and actions

Write a note to Mr Baker to explain why you should be allowed to help

Whole-class improvisation: helping in the kitchen

Mr Baker leads the children through the shop and into his kitchen. He asks them if they know what to be careful of in the kitchen and reinforces some simple safety rules. He proudly shows them around his kitchen, pointing out the shelves lined with jars of scrumptious toppings, the cupboards full of equipment and the drawers containing the utensils.

- *Can you see what's in that jar up there?*
- *Do mind those sacks of flour.*
- *What do you think I keep in my fridge?*
- *How many recipe books can you see on this shelf?*
- *Open the drawer in front of you and tell me what utensils you can see inside. Can everyone hold up a wooden spoon for me?*
- *What do we need to do before we start cooking? Why do we need to wash our hands? Turn on the tap in front of you and let me see you scrub under your nails!*
- *You'd better choose a coloured apron from this cupboard. What colour have you got? Help one another to tie the aprons. That's good.*
- *What shall we cook today? Why don't you choose your favourite bread or cake to make? I'll help you if you need me.*

The children work individually or in pairs to make their cakes and Mr Baker hobbles round giving help and advice:

- *You need some more flour in there; it's too sloppy! How many eggs are you putting in?*
- *What kind of jam are you putting in your tarts? Put the tray on that table and I will put it in the oven for you.*
- *Why don't you try making some biscuits now?*
- *When you are finished go and sit in my sitting room and help yourself to a cup of juice and a biscuit.*

When all the children are sitting down enjoying their drinks, Mr Baker sits with them and asks individuals questions about what they have made and how they got on.

 Using language to imagine; to persuade; to give reasons; to describe

Write a list of rules for safety in the kitchen

Collect recipe books

Write a recipe

Draw a picture of the kitchen and label the equipment and ingredients

Design a poster or newspaper advert advertising Mr Baker's shop

A letter arrives from the palace with a request

Teacher's intentions

- To introduce a challenge
- To make a group decision to solve the problem
- To encourage each child to make an individual contribution

Teacher in role: a request from the palace

Mr Baker hears a knock at the back door and hobbles over to open it. He finds that the postman has delivered a letter (see Figure 4.3). He holds the letter and peers at the envelope, looking scared to open it.

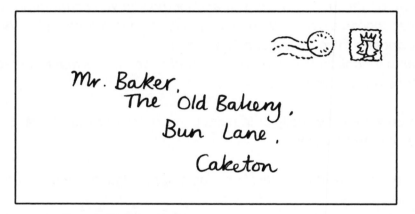

Mr. Baker,
The Old Bakery,
Bun Lane,
Caketon

Figure 4.3 The letter from the palace

- *Who do you think this is for? I don't get many letters.*
- *How do you know it's for me?*
- *Can you help me to read what it says? I haven't got my glasses.*

The letter is written by the Queen and asks Mr Baker to bake a special cake for the King's birthday (see Figure 4.4).

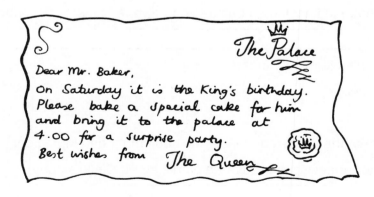

The Palace

Dear Mr. Baker,
On Saturday it is the King's birthday.
Please bake a special cake for him
and bring it to the palace at
4.00 for a surprise party.
Best wishes from   The Queen

Figure 4.4 The letter from the Queen

Mr Baker says that it is a great honour and it is a real shame that he won't be able to make the cake because of his bad back. He is very sad and sighs deeply.

Hopefully, his helpers will volunteer, but again he will need persuading that they know enough to bake such an important cake. Possible designs are discussed.

The teacher narrates the final decision, for example:,

After a great deal of discussion about the designs they decided to make a chocolate cake in the shape of a crown, with pink icing and fifty-six candles.

Reading aloud; comprehension

Persuasion; taking different views in to account; giving reasons for opinions

The cakes could be designed individually, in pairs or groups, presented and a decision made

Ritual: making the King's birthday cake

Mr Baker asks his helpers to help him make the cake. He asks them to stand in a circle around his largest mixing bowl (Imaginary!). He asks them to think of one special ingredient that they would like to put into the cake. This can be anything at all, from cherries to magic dust! We have had children wishing to add sausages and bacon to the mixture, but every offering is treated with the same respect! Individually, children drop their imaginary ingredient into the bowl and say what it is for everyone to hear. Everyone stirs the mixture together a given number of times with everyone counting loudly.

Speaking aloud individually

Write a list of ingredients used in the cake

The party

Teacher's intentions

- To explore how speech varies in formal situations;
- To give advice and share knowledge with others.

Narration and teacher in role: preparing for the big event

Narrate to the children:
The beautiful cake was baked and decorated by Mr Baker's friends. When Saturday came, Mr Baker was still too ill to go out, so he asked the children if they could take the cake to the palace for him.

Put on the apron and in role as Mr Baker say how pleased you are that the children are going to take the cake and that you are very proud of them. Ask them what they are going to wear to the party and ask whether they know the polite way of addressing the

King and Queen when they meet them. Different expressions for greeting royalty and bows/curtseys can be practised if required!

> Speaking to different people; using formal and informal language; developing an awareness of language varying in different situations

> Collect and discuss different greetings – formal and informal.
> Who would use them and when?
>
> Designing birthday cards for the King

Collective storytelling and teacher in role: the King's birthday party

Teacher narrates, with children adding detail:

The children arrived at the palace with the cake and were shown in to a huge ballroom where the party was to take place. They looked around the room and they could see ... and some golden ... (Ask individual children to supply appropriate words to describe the room) *...The children were feeling very ... as they waited. They had never met the King before but they had heard that he was ...After a while they heard footsteps approaching. They stood up and waited for the door to open.*

Tell the children that you are going to be the King in the next part of the drama. Simple costume or props can be used to indicate this change of role.

The King enters the room looking glum and holding his face. (Rub your jaw and speak as though you had a mouth full of cotton wool. Try not to make the King too similar to Mr Baker. They are both in pain but should walk and behave distinctly.)

Greet the children in a very half-hearted fashion– not rudely, but distractedly. Hopefully the children will greet the King as previously practiced; if not the King must start the conversation by groaning and asking who they are and why they are there.

The King speaks miserably, saying how kind they are but how he couldn't possibly eat any cake. He has terrible toothache.

Hopefully, the children suggest he should visit the dentist and/or brush his teeth but he has never heard of a 'Tendist' and has never used a toothbrush. (The King is unfamiliar with the word dentist and the children have to correct his mispronunciation.) He wondered why the Queen had given him a small brush and some mint-flavoured paste for his birthday. The children tell the King how to look after his teeth, advising and demonstrating correct brushing techniques. He is so pleased with the result of his clean teeth, as the brushing has dislodged something stuck between his teeth. He decides that the party can go ahead after all. The children can suggest games and sing appropriate songs (usually 'Happy Birthday!').

> Making relevant comments; include detail; explaining

> Create a poster reminding the King how to look after his teeth
>
> Make a chart or factsheet about things that are good and bad for teeth

Narration: the party is over

Ask the children to sit down and narrate the end of the story, with children adding detail.

The party was a great success and the children had a wonderful time playing (Ask individual children to suggest a game) *and ... with the King. The next day they went to tell Mr Baker all about the party and how they had helped the King to look after his teeth.*

Reflection: what have we learned?

- Who did the children help in the story?
- Was the King as they had expected him to be?
- What did they tell Mr Baker when they saw him?

 Retelling a story; recalling information; giving reasons for actions

Writing a thank you letter to the King

Making a character study for the King and the baker

Writing a letter inviting the King to visit the bakery

Set up an imaginative play corner as a bakery or the palace

Follow a recipe and bake a birthday cake

Chapter 5
The Park

The park employees meet a number of different people who all have a different impact on their lives and on the park. Ailsa, the café manager, is one of the workers, a real friend to everyone. The new path sweeper is called Botan. He lacks confidence and needs help to do his job. Ms Strindberg from the local council threatens the jobs of those who work in the park, and even the park itself. Finally, those who work in the park meet Mr Khan, who is rather lonely and has nowhere else to go every day. He is given a job in the park and makes everyone smile.

Learning objectives

- To practise talking to different people using appropriate tone and register;
- To develop a sense of citizenship;
- To interpret signs.

Themes

- Jobs
- Public spaces: parks.

Resources

- At least two puppets of any type;
- Optional costume suggestions:
  - *Ailsa* – apron, tea-towel, writing pad and paper;
  - *Botan* – gardening clothes (old coat, wellington boots, hat, scarf, gloves), broom, ball of green string, black plastic sacks;
  - *Ms Strindberg* – smart clothes, briefcase containing a large plan of the recycling centre;
  - *Mr Khan* – hat and coat (scruffy), 'secret' bag containing puppets (not to be seen until the drama takes place).

NB: The costumes do not have to be used. An appropriate prop is useful to help children distinguish between the different teacher roles.

Time

● Four sessions of thirty–forty-five minutes.

Notes

The imaginative play area can be designed as the park.

Figure 5.1 The park

Meeting Ailsa

Teacher's intentions

● To establish the context of the drama;
● To enable the children to create their own place in the pretend world;
● To introduce the character of Ailsa.

Creating roles: who's who

Tell the children that the drama today is going to be about a park. Share experiences and knowledge of parks.

● *What would you find in a park?*
● *What do you like doing there?*
● *What jobs would the people who work there have?*

Tell the children they are going to do some drama about a park and they are all going to pretend to be the people who work in the park. Children decide what jobs they would like to do in the park.

Freeze frames and thought tapping: at work in the park

Individually or in small groups, children make pictures of jobs being done in the park. The children hold their positions to depict the job they are doing in the park while the teacher taps the children in turn and asks questions. Examples are:

● *Can you tell me what are you doing today in the park?*
● *What tools are you using?*
● *Is that tiring?*

Make a list of jobs in the park (e.g. water the plants, sell ice creams, cut the grass)

Narration and dramatic play: a normal day in the park

Tell the children that the park will be brought to life and that they will be able to move about and speak to each other. Tell them you are going to be a person called Ailsa who works in the café and will be joining in with them. It is useful to wear an apron or carry a prop such as a tea-towel to indicate when you are in role.

Ask them to return to the freeze frame and then start to narrate:

One sunny day in the park, all the people who were employed there were working very hard. Ailsa, the lady who worked in the café, was going around the park and asking everyone what kind of sandwiches they wanted for their lunches.

Ailsa walks around the park chatting to the workers and making a list of sandwich requirements. Minor incidents may arise (instigated by Ailsa or as a natural result of the workers interacting in the park, e.g. a lost dog, the mower runs out of petrol, it starts to rain).

In role discussion: what happened to you today?

Ailsa gathers the workers together and they sit down to discuss what has been happening in the park today.

● *What were you doing today?*
● *What kind of sandwich did you have for lunch?*
● *Did the dog do any damage?*

Children draw an individual picture of something they would like to see in the park or of themselves working in the park. These can be stuck onto a large piece of paper to create a collective montage.

Meeting Botan

Teacher's intentions

● To introduce simple costumes or props to build up an impression of the role;
● To develop the children's roles;

- To give children experience of giving advice through interacting with teacher in role;
- To give the children practice in describing and explaining.

Costuming: preparing the teacher in role

If you are using the bag of props/costumes, place them in the middle of the circle of seated children. Tell the children that in the story about the park they are going to meet someone new who has never been to the park before. This person owns the bag in the middle and they are going to find out more about them by taking out one thing at a time and seeing if they can guess anything about the visitor.

Invite the children one at a time to take items out of the bag and lay them on the floor. As each item of clothing or prop is removed, ask questions to draw out the children's understanding:

- *Who do think would wear a hat like this?*
- *Why are they carrying a ball of green string?*
- *What do we use a broom like this for?*
- *What is this?*

Tell the children that you are going to pretend to be the person who owns these things. Dress in the clothes and/or hold the props as appropriate. The children can help you to dress if you feel comfortable.

The children go back into their spaces where they were doing their work as before. Tell them that the new person will be arriving soon and that they will see him arrive.

 Prediction, description, use of vocabulary

Whole-group improvisation: meeting Botan

Go to the door and return slowly in role as Botan. Perhaps develop a slight stoop and rub your back occasionally to give the impression that you are quite old and creaky.

Hello everyone. I'm looking for Flower Park. Am I in the right place? Do you all work here?

Chat with the park workers and introduce yourself. Tell them that you have been employed as a new path sweeper and haven't done this kind of work before. You need an outside job because of your asthma. Can they tell you what happens here and what you will have to do? Try to portray Botan as rather vulnerable but kind.

Encourage the children tell Botan about the park and show him around. They may introduce him to everyone and show him where to find his tools and where to have a cup of tea.

 Talking in role, giving information and instructions

Draw and label pictures of Botan

Draw a collective map of the park. Children draw themselves on to the map and label

Discussion: what did we think of Botan?

Talk about Botan and discuss what they thought about him.

- *What kind of person was he?*
- *Why had he come to the park?*
- *What did you help him to do?*
- *How do you think he will get on with his job? Will he be good at it?*
- *Which words or phrases describe Botan's impact on the park?*

 Giving opinions, describing events, expressing viewpoints

Meeting Ms Strindberg

Teacher's intentions

- To introduce a more confrontational role;
- To encourage children to develop skills of persuasion and argue a case in role;
- To see something from different points of view.

Costuming: preparing the teacher role

Place the new bag of props in the middle of the circle of seated children.

Tell the children that in the story about the park today, they are going to meet another person who has never been to the park before. This person owns the bag in the middle of the circle and they are going to find out more about the person by taking out one thing at a time and seeing what they can guess about who they are going to meet today.

As before, invite the children one at a time to take things out of the bag and lay them on the floor. As each item of clothing or prop is removed, ask questions to draw out the children's understanding.

- *Who do think would wear a hat like this?*
- *Why do people carry briefcases?*
- *Is this person smart, casual or scruffy?*

Whole-group improvisation: Ms Strindberg brings news

Tell the children that in the story you are going to pretend to be the person who owns these things. Dress in the clothes or hold the props as appropriate. Tell them that the new person will be arriving soon and that this time they are all having a tea break in the café when the person arrives. Give children a minute to sit in the café and start handing out imaginary cups of tea.

Go over to the door and walk back smartly and purposefully. You smile very falsely at everyone and speak with a slightly superior tone. Ms Strindberg is a very bossy and officious woman.

Good afternoon everyone. My name is Ms Strindberg. I'm from the council. Are you all the people who work here in the park? I need to have a chat with you about something very important. Can I sit down here? Good. Now then, I expect you've all heard that the council has been looking for a place to build a new recycling centre. People are so careful these days to recycle their cans and bottles, and the council wants to build a shiny new building where all the things can be collected and the recycled. They have chosen this park as the best place to build the centre and I've brought the plans here today to show you.

Take the plans out of your briefcase and show them to the workers. By now they will be asking lots of questions and may even be shouting at Ms Strindberg that it is not fair that their park has been chosen. Ms Strindberg deals with this reaction by asking them for their ideas and saying she will report back to the council with their viewpoint. She is only the messenger and can't make any decisions herself.

 Ask and answer questions, persuade, give reasons for and against

Meeting and discussion: what do you think of the plans?

Ask children to discuss in pairs what they think about the proposals. There may be mixed reactions to the news.
Teacher in role as Ailsa leads a discussion with all the workers:

- *What did we think of Ms Strindberg and her ideas?*
- *What was Ms Strindberg like?*
- *What was the council going to do?*
- *Did they agree with the plans?*
- *Why are recycling facilities needed?*
- *What could the workers do to stop the recycling centre being built in their park?*

This drama can finish in a number of different ways depending on the reactions and suggestions of the children. The story must end to satisfy the workers/children. Possible endings include:

- Narrating that after the protests the council changed their mind and built the recycling centre elsewhere;
- Receiving a letter from the council, which can be read to the workers;
- Workers make protest banners and march to the council offices (around the classroom or playground) and meet the leader of the council, who is persuaded to rethink the plans.

 Put forward an argument for or against

Making posters: 'Save our Park'

Writing a petition against the park closure

Writing a newspaper article

Improvising a television or radio interview between a park worker and TV reporter

Meeting Mr Khan

Teacher's intentions

- To encourage children to interact with a character who is lonely and miserable in role;
- To practise using supportive and encouraging language;
- To introduce an element of surprise when the bag of puppets is revealed.

Costuming: preparing the teacher's role

Place the next bag of props in the middle of the circle of seated children. Tell the children that they are going to meet a third person, who they have seen very often in the park, always sitting on the same bench and looking sad. This person owns the bag in the middle of the circle and they are going to find out more about the person by taking out one thing at a time, as before:

- *Who do think would wear a hat like this?*
- *Why do you think he looks so sad?*
- *Is this person smart or scruffy?*
- *I wonder what is inside this bag. Perhaps we'll find out when we meet the person who owns it*

Tell the children that in the story you are going to pretend to be the person who owns these things. Dress in the clothes or hold the props as appropriate. Ask the children to give the person a name – we've called him Mr Khan.

Whole-group improvisation: learning about Mr Khan

Tell the children that you will be Mr Khan and will be sitting on the bench in the park. The park workers have decided to speak to the man and find out why he looks so miserable and fed up. Decide what might be an opening line and ask for a volunteer to approach Mr Khan and begin the conversation.

Mr Khan responds in a very miserable voice, slowly giving out information:

- *I live alone*
- *I come to the park every day to look at the birds and feed the ducks*
- *I watch the children playing and remember when I used to work in this park many years ago*

Hopefully the children will want to know what Mr Khan used to do. He was a puppeteer and put on puppet shows in the park for the children. He thinks that children these days are not interested in puppets and he hasn't done a show for years. With encouragement, he opens his secret bag to reveal a selection of puppets and is persuaded to do a show for the park workers. They may ask him to come again and do regular shows for the children.

Discussion: what do we know about Mr Khan?

Talk about Mr Khan and what the children thought of him.

- *Was he a nice person?*
- *Why had he come to the park?*
- *What did you do to help him?*

Story circle: ending the story

To end the story of the park, ask the children to sit in a circle and take it in turns to add a sentence to tell the story of what happens to the characters we have met in the park. You may provide some link sentences to keep the story going and to bring different parts together.

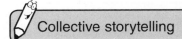 Collective storytelling

Make puppets and stage a puppet show

Read stories about parks (e.g. *Percy the Park Keeper* by Nick Butterworth)

Reflection: what have we learned?

- *How did we feel about each of the different people we met?*

Encourage the children to compare the four characters they met in the park. How did each character change the atmosphere in the park? (e.g. Ms Strindberg made them angry; Botan made them happy).

Figure 5.2 Park scene by Beth

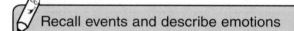

Recall events and describe emotions

Make a list of words and phrases to describe them (e.g. Ailsa – friendly, nice, happy; Botan – nervous, needed help, had a bad back)

Retell the story of when Ms Strindberg or Mr Khan came to the park

Chapter 6
The Sun Wizard

The people of a small village are preparing for a very important event that is to take place in the evening when it is dark. However, on the evening of the event, darkness refuses to fall for the first time ever. The surprised villagers receive a letter from the Sun Wizard. He tells them that he has cast a special spell, preventing the sun from ever setting again. What can the villagers do to solve the problem? Together they confront the wizard who turns out to be afraid of the dark, especially the noises he hears when he is in bed. Can the villagers persuade him to change his mind and see that the dark is not really frightening when you know what is making the noises?

Learning objectives

- To understand the importance of and need for day and night;
- To identify different light sources, including the sun.

Themes

- Light and dark/day and night.

Resources

- Letter or scroll from the Sun Wizard (text provided, see Figure 6.3 p. 45);
- Large paper or whiteboard and pens;
- Cloak or prop for the wizard.

Time

- Two hours – can be divided in to shorter sessions.

What do we know about day and night?

Teacher's intentions

- Establishing understanding of day and night;
- Clarifying human relationships with light and dark.

Discussion: introducing ideas about day and night

Tell the children that the story they are going to tell is about day and night. Ask the children to think about things that take place at night and things that happen during the day when it is light. These things can be listed on to a large sheet of paper divided in to two columns (see Figure 6.1). Alternatively, the children could be given pictures of daytime and night activities to sort into the two sets.

Day ☀	Night ✶ ☾✶
Wake up	Sleep
Get dressed	Wear pyjamas
Go to school	Have a bath
Shopping	Watch TV
Play in the garden	Go to parties
Beach	Santa comes
Birds fly	Fireworks
Animals eat and play	Owls wake up
	Nocturnal animals like badgers and foxes come out
Sun	Moon and stars

Figure 6.1 An example list of things that happen during the day and at night

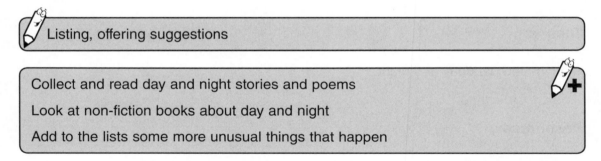

Listing, offering suggestions

Collect and read day and night stories and poems

Look at non-fiction books about day and night

Add to the lists some more unusual things that happen

Mime: activities in the day

Take one or two examples of daytime activities that we do, suggested by the children, and mime the activities as a whole group. Examples are: waking up in the morning, walking to school, playing football, flying a kite, hanging out the washing, shopping. Encourage the children to think carefully about the mime, their movements, and also gesture and facial expression.

- *How do we walk to school?*
- *Are we happy skipping along like this?*

Demonstrate and encourage all of the children to copy you.

- *Sometimes we might drag our heels like this.*

Again, encourage the children to copy your mime.

- *Now you show me how you walk to school/the park.*

The children choose a way they prefer and mime their walk.

Freeze frames and thought tapping: actions of day and night

Introduce the 'freeze' control. Ask the children to do their mimes and then stop on the instruction '1-2-3 freeze!' Tell them that this looks like a picture that could come from a storybook. The special thing is that with this picture you are able to speak to the people in the picture by touching them one at a time on the shoulder. Demonstrate this with a few children asking questions appropriate to their position. Questions should be differentiated according to the children's confidence and ability. The questions on this list demand different levels of response.

- *What are you doing on this lovely day?*
- *What clothes are you putting on?*
- *Where are you standing?*
- *Are you on your own or are you fishing with your friends?*
- *How long does it take you to walk to school?*
- *Why are you looking so gloomy?*
- *Is it a sunny day?*
- *What will you do in the park?*
- *Can you see anyone else on the beach?*
- *I can see you are holding something. Can you tell me what it is?*
- *What does the sand feel like under your feet?*

Another special thing is that when you clap the people in the picture start to move and the mimes can continue.

Now choose a couple of night activities to mime and encourage the children to join in as before. Examples are: watching fireworks, holding sparklers, looking at the stars and the moon, getting ready for bed. These night mimes can again be frozen and individuals questioned as before.

 Answering questions; selecting relevant detail

 Children collect pictures or photographs of things happening in the day or at night and write captions

Dramatic play: activities of the day and night

Tell the children that this time they will be able to talk when they are doing their activities. They can talk to one another or to themselves. (Some begin by making noises and not interacting with others, but this is fine.)

Choose either the day or night activities to explore in this way.

 Speaking in role

Setting the scene

Teacher's intentions

● To create the context of the story;
● To develop a village community.

Mime, freeze frame with thought tap and narration: meeting the villagers

Tell the children that you are going to start to tell the story and that they are going to help you by being the people in the story. Tell them to choose one of the day activities to mime and after a few seconds freeze the picture as they did earlier. Narrate the following:

Once, in a place very far from here there was a little village. In the village there lived all kinds of different people. If you walked through the village on a sunny day you would be sure to see the villagers out and about doing lots of different things.

Talk to the children about the things they are doing in the village today. Ask children to choose a role for themselves.

● *Where are you in the village today?*
● *What are you doing?*
● *What are you carrying in your heavy bag?*
● *What is your dog called?*
● *Can you tell me what buildings you can see around you?*
● *Do you live near the market place?*
● *What are you planting in your garden?*
● *Are you on your way to the shop? What will you buy?*

Indicate again that the image can come to life as a mime when you clap your hands. Leave the mime to run for a few seconds and then freeze it again.

Now ask the children to do their chosen night mime. Start them off and then after a few seconds give the freeze command and narrate the following:

The people all loved to be out in the sunshine during the day but also loved the evening time. It was then that they could do all the things that they enjoyed doing when it was dark. Some of them liked to ...

Touch a few individuals on the shoulder and ask them to say what they enjoy doing in the dark.

Describing fictional characters and settings

Responding to narrative

Children decide on a character for themselves in the village. They draw pictures of their characters. They write something about their own character

Draw a map of the village. Draw a picture of houses and people in the village. Indicate where the owl's nest and badger's set are. Label the village pond, wood, road, church. Give the village a name

Find out about light sources, natural and artificial

Find out information about the sun, the moon and stars

A big Shining Sun by phoebe

Figure 6.2 A big shining Sun by Phoebe

Introductions in role: meeting the villagers

You have to make certain decisions in this session about the choice of event that is the focus of the session. Decide on a special event that is going to take place in the village. You could ask the children to suggest what could be happening. This event can only happen in the dark, e.g. a special bonfire party/ switching on the Christmas lights, or a barbecue.

Hopefully, the children will have had the opportunity to think about the person that they are going to be in the story before this session starts. If not, ask them to decide now.

Ask all the villagers to introduce themselves to the rest of the group.

Organize and what they say and focus on the main points

Teacher in role: the village celebration is prepared

The teacher takes on role of an enthusiastic woman. She asks them about preparations for the exciting event to come. They are all getting ready for what was going to take place that very evening. Everyone has a special job to do to get the party ready.

Ask the villagers what kind of things they will have to do to prepare for the party. For example:

- making food
- putting up decorations
- building the bonfire
- organizing music.

Depending on the age and experience of the children, select one of the following ways of improvising the scene:

(a) Ask the children to choose something to do to help get the party ready and improvise the scene. Ask them to tell you what it is they have chosen to do. In this improvisation you will go round chatting and giving advice about what needs doing:

- *Now, have you got everything you need?*
- *Will we have enough sandwiches?*
- *Who is in charge of the fairy lights?*
- *Did anyone buy any sparklers?*
- *Can someone help me with this table?*

(b) For inexperienced groups, lead the children in improvising with everyone making food or putting up decorations together:

- *Let's start with putting up the fairy lights. Everyone get some out of this box. Be careful with them because they're very delicate. Stretch up like this and hang them on the hooks like this. I'll just turn them on to test that they're working. That looks brilliant. I'll turn them off now until it gets dark. We need it to be dark so that we can see the lights in all their glory. What's next? Oh yes, the food ...*

> Draw pictures with captions/annotations or write about jobs done to prepare the party
>
> Design posters advertising the event

Night doesn't fall

Teacher's intentions

- Introducing the problem.

Narration, letter and discussion: why won't it get dark?

Before the session starts, hide the scroll or the envelope containing the letter from the Sun Wizard (see Figure 6.3) in a strategic place to be retrieved at the appropriate moment. Ask the children to remember where they were standing in the village and take up positions again, and narrate:

After a great deal of hard work the party was ready. Everyone changed into their best clothes and sat down to wait for it to get dark so that the party could begin. They waited and waited and waited but the sun stayed high in the sky. It was getting very late, but still the sun did not go down and the sky was still blue and very bright. Whatever could have happened?

Teacher in role gathers the villagers to talk about what has happened.

- *What can have happened?*
- *Has anyone got any ideas?*

Invite some speculation but cut this short by announcing:

- *I just saw someone quietly creep up and drop something over there. It seems to be a message of some kind.*

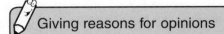

Giving reasons for opinions

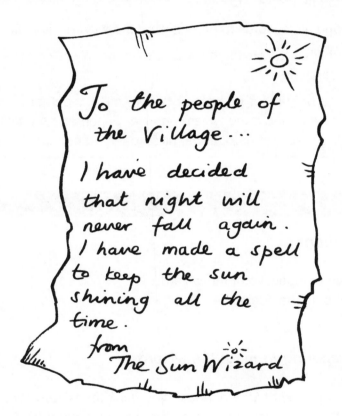

Figure 6.3 The letter from the Sun Wizard

Whole-group improvisation and discussion: a letter arrives

Pick up the scroll or envelope from the hiding place (see Figure 6.3). Read the letter or invite someone to help with the reading. It says that the sun will not set again because he has cast a spell to prevent it.

- *What will we do if it never gets dark again?*
- *What things will not be able to happen?*
- *What can be done about this problem?*
- *Has anyone ever heard about this Sun Wizard before?*
- *Where does he live? Is there an address on the letter?*

If the children do not suggest it then you will need to say:

- *Should we try to talk to him and see if we can find out why he's cast this spell?*
- *What will we say to the wizard?*
- *How will we persuade him to change the spell?*
- *What will happen if he won't talk to us?*
- *Perhaps we should write a letter to take with us and then if he won't see us we can put it through the letterbox.*

 Ask questions to clarify understanding

Write a letter to the wizard with reasons why he should change his spell

List questions to ask the wizard

Draw pictures and write words to predict what the wizard will look like

Draw pictures of what they think the wizard's house might look like. Add annotations or captions

Use a large piece or number of pieces of paper stuck together to create an outline map of how to get to the wizards house. Encourage the children to draw features on to the map – stream, trees, hills, roads – and label it

Meeting the Sun Wizard

Teacher's intentions

- To consider the perspective of the wizard;
- To think about personal fears.

Discussion: preparing to meet the wizard

- *Can you remember what kind of house you think the wizard lives in?*
- *What do you think the wizard might be like when we meet him?*
- *How will he react to our arrival?*
- *What will we say when we first meet him?*
- *Let's read our letter(s) or go over our list of questions* (if these were done as an additional activity).

 Prediction, description, framing questions

Whole-group improvisation: the journey to the wizard's house

Teacher in role leads the villagers on an imaginary journey describing features as they go as an additional activity. Use a map if one was made as an additional activity.

- *Which way do we go?*

It works well if you can lead the children out of the class and across the playground or through the hall. This makes the journey even more exciting and memorable.

- *Be careful of this tree-trunk; pick your feet up high.*
- *Watch out for the snake pit. Jump over the stream.*

When you feel the journey has been completed, stop the children and gather them together.

- *We've arrived outside the wizard's house. What can you see? Isn't it bright?*

Ask individuals to describe what they can see in front of them. Encourage children to talk about bright colours, lights blazing etc.

Teacher in role: an important meeting

Tell the children that in the next part of the story you are going to be the wizard. You will be in your house. Agree how you will know that the villagers have arrived. Will they knock?

On the agreed signal greet the villagers. The wizard is very nervous and jumpy. Make sure you give enough time for the children to respond to you.

- *Hello everyone. Who are you? I don't get many visitors. Welcome to my home. Would you like to come in?*
- *Please sit down.*
- *What is it you wanted?*
- *Oh yes, the spell ... Well I'm sorry but you won't make me change my mind. There is no way I am going to let it get dark again.*

Through comments and questions, enable the villagers to tell the wizard about the celebration they have planned. Also invite them to tell you about the other things that only happen at night through questions such as:

- *Why is night so important anyway?*
- *But surely all of these things can happen in the light, and the badgers and foxes will soon get used to waking up in the light, won't they?*

Eventually, the Wizard confesses:

- *I hate the dark. I just can't take anymore.*

Let the villagers question the wizard. Don't give too much information away at once. Eventually, tell the villagers that there are too many horrible frightening things at night. You haven't been able to sleep properly for weeks with the 'twit twoooo' noise outside. Then there is the tapping on the bedroom window, the one on the forest side of your bedroom. You can't see in the dark and it's frightening.

Eventually, let the villagers persuade you that the noises are all easily explained and it will be a disaster for so many animals, plants and people if it never gets dark again.

Finish the session by saying:

Well, I suppose you're right. You have made me feel better about the dark. I know that it's only an owl sitting on the tree outside my window and hooting and I know that the branch scratches my window when the wind blows. Thank you for explaining all these things to me. And you're right about all of the animals too.

I'll have to make a new spell to change things again. I think I'll need your help for this special spell. I would like you all to think of a magic word to say to make the spell work. It should be a long and interesting word that sounds exciting. Do you think you can all find a word like that? It doesn't have to be a magic word like 'abracadabra' but one that sounds good like 'supersonic' or 'fabulous'. These kinds of words have a lot of magic power.

Take off the cloak and indicate that the meeting with the wizard is over for today.

Framing and responding to questions

Persuasive language

Vocabulary extension

Write a list of fears about the dark

Discussion: help for the wizard

Out of role, discuss the wizard and his problems. Is there anything else the children could suggest to make him feel better?

Write advice on Post-it notes to help the wizard be brave

Draw pictures of the meeting with the wizard. Add speech bubbles or thought bubbles to the characters

Decide on the magic word to use in the spell. Write a list of magic words/make up some new ones

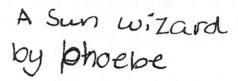

Figure 6.4 A Sun Wizard by Phoebe

The celebration goes ahead

Teacher's intentions

● To enable the children to evaluate the effectiveness of their suggestions;
● To provide a fun and satisfying ending to the drama.

Teacher in role and narration: night falls

In this final session the children help the wizard to make a spell and invite him to join them in their celebration. Ask the children to stand in a circle. Teacher in role as the Sun Wizard says:

Thank you all so much for coming to see me this evening. You've really helped me to see how silly I've been. Now let's see if we can work together and make a reversing spell. Have you all thought of a word? Good.

Invite the villagers one at a time to say their word. Write the word on to a Post-it and stick it onto a large sheet of paper.

Tell the children to close their eyes. Count to three. Clap.

Open your eyes, everyone. The spell's worked! Well done. The sun is beginning to go down and you will be able to have your party. Don't let me hold you up.

Hopefully, the villagers will invite the wizard. He will need a little persuading, but will be happy to go. If session time allows, improvise the party. Alternatively, finish the session with narration:

The people of the village had a wonderful party and the wizard enjoyed himself very much. He was still rather worried about sleeping in the dark but his new friends told him again not to be afraid and to leave the light on for the time being if he was feeling a little scared. And that is the end of our story about the villagers and the Sun Wizard.

 Shared storytelling

Reflection: what have we learned?

Ask the children to stand in a circle. Ask the children to come forward one at a time to say something about the wizard. Examples can be given by the teacher to give the children ideas:

- *I liked the wizard.*
- *He was sad and we helped him.*
- *He was frightened of the dark.*
- *He made a spell.*

Discuss the story. Recap on the reasons for the wizard's fear of the dark and discuss the explanations given by the villagers. Discuss why light and dark are important for our world. Perhaps go on to discuss the children's own fears, if appropriate.

- *Are there times when you have been scared of something?*
- *What did you do?*

 Making suggestions, giving reasons for opinions

Retell the story of the wizard in a story circle. Sequencing events and adding detail

Write the story of the Sun Wizard

Chapter 7
Beside the Seaside

The beach is a lovely place for children to come and play. The people who work there meet a number of different characters who have various problems to solve. Mai Ling is a little girl who is afraid of the water. Mal is looking after the donkeys for her sick uncle and needs help. Georgie is doing too much sunbathing and is getting very burnt. Let's hope the children can sort them out!

Learning objectives

- To solve problems in different ways;
- To use different language registers;
- To develop prediction skills.

Themes

- The seaside
- Helping others
- Personal health and safety
- Fears.

Resources – optional costume suggestions:

- *Mai Ling* – swimming kit, goggles, towel, teddy, bucket and spade, arm bands or a rubber ring, shells;
- *Mal* – book about donkeys, bucket and shovel, old coat;
- *Georgie* – towel, suntan lotion, sunhat, empty bottle of water, T-shirt, sunglasses.

NB: The props do not have to be used but really enhance the children's experience in the drama.

Time

- Four sessions of thirty minutes.

Notes

Consider linking this drama with a visit to the seaside. The imaginative play area can be designed as the beach or perhaps the travel agents. Make a large frieze of a beach scene as a backdrop to the imaginative play area.

The beach is a lovely place to work

Teacher's intentions

- To build commitment to the beach setting;
- To develop individual roles.

Discussion: setting the scene

- *Who has been on holiday?*
- *Was it in this country or abroad?*

Talk about day trips or holidays on the beach. Tell the children that they are going to do some drama about a beach. Ask the children to discuss with a partner what they know about beaches. What have they done on the beach? Lead a class discussion:

- *What do you see and hear if you are at the beach?*
- *What do people do there?*
- *What jobs do people do who work on or near the beach?*

Tell the children they are going to pretend to be the people who work at the beach in our drama today. The children decide what jobs they would like to do on the beach (e.g. rent out deckchairs to people on the beach, sell ice-creams, paint beach huts, run the Punch and Judy show). It is a good idea for everyone to introduce themselves and say what job they do. Children can identify others who are doing the same job to work with.

Discussion, sharing personal experiences, including relevant detail

Read or tell stories about the beach. These could be anecdotal

Collect non-fiction and fiction books about the seaside to display

Look at pictures of different beaches

Make a list of things you might see (e.g. deck chairs, pier, beach huts, ice-cream stall, donkey rides)

Make a list of the kinds of jobs people do at the beach

Freeze frames, thought tapping and dramatic play: creating the beach

Ask the children to find a space in the room. They may be on their own or in pairs or small groups. Ask the children to freeze when you say 'one, two, three, freeze', and show a freeze frame of jobs being done on the beach. This is like a postcard of a beach scene. Thought tap the workers about what they are doing.

- *What are you doing today?*
- *Have you worked here for long?*
- *What's the weather like here today?*
- *Have you had many visitors today?*
- *Is the sea cold?*

Clap your hands to bring the beach to life. Wander around chatting to the people and finding out what's happening on the beach today. Encourage the children to make up their own stories and join in with their play.

 Talking in role

Write lists of what you can you see, hear, smell, taste and touch at the seaside

Draw an outline of a suitcase. Draw pictures of items you would pack to take on holiday. Label the items

Meeting Mai Ling, who is scared of the sea

Teacher's intentions

- To introduce the teacher in role as Mai Ling;
- For the children to use their knowledge and be able to give comfort and reassurance to someone in distress;
- To be able to use persuasive language.

Costuming and preparing the teacher in role: Mai Ling is introduced

If props are being used, place the bag in the middle of the circle of seated children. Tell them that in the story about the beach today, they are going to meet someone new who has never been to the beach before. Her name is Mai Ling. She owns the bag in the middle and they are going to find out more about her by taking out one item at a time and seeing if they can make guesses about her, such as how old she is and what she likes doing.

Invite children one at a time to take items out of the bag and lay them on the floor. As each item of clothing or prop is removed from the bag, ask questions to draw out the children's understanding:

- *Why would she need a towel?*
- *What are the goggles used for?*

- *What do the arm bands tell us about her?*
- *How old do you think she is?*

Tell the children that in the story you are going to be the little girl called Mai Ling who is about five years old. Arrange the props around you or hold some of them as appropriate. Tell the children that they are going to meet Mai Ling and hear her speak but are not able to talk to her at the moment.

 Listening to focus on detail

Teacher in role: monologue of Mai Ling

In role as Mai Ling, sit down, holding the teddy tightly, and look around you nervously.

Oh dear. I've never been to the beach before. It's so big. My brothers and sisters have gone off down to the sea for a swim but I'm too scared. They say it's fun, but I don't think so at all. It looks cold and wet and there are scary waves to knock me over. And I don't like the sand. It sticks to my feet.

Discussion and hot seating: talking to Mai Ling

Put down the teddy and talk to the children as teacher.

- *What have they heard?*
- *Why is Mai Ling looking so upset?*
- *What could the people who work on the beach say to her to cheer her up and give her confidence?*

The workers then talk to the teacher in role as Mai Ling about her worries. They try to reassure her that things are not really scary, but exciting and fun. They can also give her advice about keeping safe on the beach (e.g. not going into the water on her own or when the waves are big).

 Talk to teacher in role using appropriate sympathetic tone and register

Whole group improvisation: reassuring Mai Ling

The workers could show Mai Ling around the beach and introduce themselves. They could lead her down to the water's edge and teach her to paddle or jump over the waves. They could show her how to skim stones across the water or build a sandcastle.
   They will need to reassure her when she is nervous and says things like:

- *I'm worried I might fall into the water and drown.*
- *Why is the sea so big?*
- *I'm frightened about what I might tread on.*
- *What are these shell things for?*

- *How do you make sure the sand sticks together to make a castle?*
- *I haven't got a flag. What else could I stick on the top?*

They could also teach her about the dangers of the sea and how to stay safe.

- *Should I just run straight in?*
- *I could lie down and let the sea cover me up. Would I be able to breathe?*

After a while Mai Ling thanks the workers for their help and says she feels much better now. She is happy to play on the edge and wait for her family without feeling nervous and knowing how to stay safe.

Talking to teacher in role giving instructions and explanations

Make a poster about safety in the water

Identify, draw and label creatures that can be found on the beach (e.g. crabs, seagulls)

Discussion: what do we think of Mai Ling?

Talk about Mai Ling and what the children thought of her.

- *Was she a nice person?*
- *Why had she come to the beach?*
- *Why was she scared?*
- *What did you help her to do?*
- *How did she feel after we had shown her around?*
- *What did she learn?*
- *What could she do now? – e.g. learn to swim.*

Look at a map and identify different beaches. Put flags on the map to indicate where the children have visited. Talk about and identify other geographical features identified on maps that are found on beaches (e.g. caves, rivers, dunes)

Collective drawing: we were there! Children draw an individual picture of something they would like to the beach or a picture of themselves working or playing on the beach. These may be stuck on to a large sheet of paper to create a collective montage. Use a digital camera to take pictures of the children's faces. These may be stuck on to the children's self-portraits so that everyone can appear in the collective picture

Meeting Mal, who has a four-legged problem

Teacher's intentions

- To introduce a new teacher role with a new problem;
- To use the children's knowledge to solve the problem.

Costuming: preparing the teacher role

Place the next bag of props in the middle of the circle of seated children. Tell the children that in the story about the beach today, they are going to meet another person whom they have never met before. This person owns the bag in the middle and they are going to find out more about the person by taking out one item at a time and seeing if they can guess who it is going to be this time.

As before, invite the children one at a time to take items out of the bag and lay them on the floor. As each item of clothing or prop is removed, ask questions to draw out the children's understandings.

Tell the children that in the story you are going to pretend to be the person who owns these things. Dress in the clothes or hold the props as you choose. Ask the children to give the person a name – we will call her Mal.

Tell them that you will be Mal and she will be arriving in a few minutes.

> Write a list of things to do on the beach to keep you busy (e.g. build a sand castle or sand car, have a competition to see how many buckets of water you can fill in a minute do beach exercises or throw pebbles into a bucket)

Discussion and improvisation: Mal needs some help

The children, again in role as beach workers, are approached by teacher in role as Mal who begins a conversation. Mal is a lively, jolly lady who is in a spot of bother.

> *My uncle is Mr Atkins, who owns the donkeys, and he has been taken ill. I've come down to the beach to look after the donkeys and run the donkey ride business, but I'm not sure what to do. I've never looked after any animals before.*
>
> *Can you help me by advising how to feed, groom and exercise the donkeys? Can you show me how to brush this donkey? Should I do it like this? Is this right?*
>
> *What do I need this bucket and shovel for?*

If appropriate, a book on animals or the internet could be used to access information about correct approaches, but as long as the ideas are reasonable it is probably better to accept the children's suggestions.

Whole group improvisation: helping Mal

Mal asks for their help to look after the donkeys. Groups of children could be given one donkey each to name and look after. They could feedback to the whole group about any problems they may have had.

> Giving advice using appropriate tone and register

> Information retrieval; find out about donkeys. Find information for keeping a donkey healthy
>
> Stand in water or sand and describe how it feels. Collect vocabulary

Discussion: what do we think of Mal?

Talk about Mal and what they thought of her.

- *Was she a busy person?*
- *Why had she come to the beach?*
- *What did you help her to do?*

Meeting Georgie, who is hot and bothered

Teacher's intentions

- To give advice and guidance to the teacher in role;
- To use argument, giving alternatives, listening to alternative viewpoints;
- To raise issues about safety in the sun.

Costuming: preparing the teacher role – meeting Georgie

Place the next bag of props in the middle of the circle of seated children. Tell the children that in the story about the beach today they are going to meet another person who they have never met before. This person owns the bag in the middle and they are going to find out more about the person by taking out one item at a time.

As before, invite the children one at a time to take items out of the bag and lay them out on the floor. As each item of clothing or prop is removed, ask questions to draw out the children's understanding.

Tell the children that in the story you are going to pretend to be the person who owns these things. Dress in the clothes or hold the props as you choose. Ask the children to give the person a name – we will call the person Georgie, and he or she can be male or female. Tell them that you will be Georgie and will be arriving in a few minutes. They are to watch what happens and then will talk about what they have seen Georgie do.

Teacher in role: monologue of Georgie

Unroll the towel and lie down, fan your face, sigh, shuffle around as if feeling uncomfortable.

The sun's really hot today. I've been lying here for hours. I am feeling really strange. My skin is burning and I've got a headache. I wonder why I'm feeling like this. I'm really thirsty but I didn't bring a drink with me. I feel sick.

Discussion: what have we learned about Georgie?

Why is Georgie feeling bad? Try to get the children to tell you about the dangers of being out in the sun for too long and what you need to do to prevent dehydration and burning.

Georgie has all the necessary clothing and equipment in the bag and the children will hopefully refer to the hat, the water and the suntan lotion. Tell the children that they are going to have the chance to speak to Georgie about it.

Whole group improvisation: advising Georgie

Hello everyone. I wonder if you could help me. I'm feeling a bit poorly. I've been sunbathing for a few hours and I want to get a good tan. Wearing a hat is silly. Mum gave me this one and I feel stupid. If I put cream on it might go in my eyes or make my hands all sticky. I've heard people say 'Slip, slap, slop.' I've wondered what it meant. Do you know?

Workers offer advice to Georgie about ways to avoid burning by wearing a hat and a T-shirt and to avoid headaches by drinking water.

 Use of persuasive language

Find out about safety on the beach. Talk about the coastguards and how to contact them in an emergency. Talk about not eating before swimming, currents and the danger of falling rocks. Make a safety poster

Children can design a selection of beachwear for themselves (e.g. a towel, a sunhat, a swimsuit, sunglasses, a beach bag). Labels can be added

Reflection: what have we learned?

Talk about Georgie and what the workers thought about the sunbathing.

- *What advice did you give?*
- *Did you change Georgie's point of view?*
- *How did we interact with the other people we met?*
- *Did we make a difference to them?*
- *Did talking to them teach us anything or make us think differently?*

Chapter 8
The Toymaker's Workshop

The toymaker makes wonderful toys for children. She is getting so many orders for her toys that she needs to employ more staff to work with her. Tonica the toymaker and her apprentices (the children) design and make new toys, but they also mend old toys that are worn out. They meet Charlie Bear, who was once a much-loved bear but now sits alone on a shelf covered in dust. Charlie Bear's owner now has new toys to play with and he is feeling very neglected. They also receive a visit from a representative for a large toy company (or Father Christmas, if it is an appropriate time of the year), who wants designs for some new traditional toys. Can the apprentices rise to these challenges?

Learning objectives

- To understand care and responsibilities;
- To provide problem-solving opportunities;
- To use a range of different speaking registers.

Themes

- Helping others
- Toys.

Resources – optional

- Costume suggestions: Tonica the toymaker – overall or apron, clipboard and pen; *Charlie Bear* – brown coat, scarf, gloves; *Rupert* – briefcase, large letter addressed to the toymaker (see Figure 8.2 p. 60);
- Large sheet of paper and felt-tip pens;
- Art materials.

Time

- One hour.

Notes

The imaginative play area can be designed as the toymaker's workshop.

Figure 8.1

Resource

TOBY'S TOY SHOP

Dear Tonica,

We have heard that you are a wonderful toymaker.

We would like you to design and make some new toys that could be sold in our shop. We already have enough electronic toys and ones that use batteries. We really want some old-fashioned toys. Toys that you push and pull would be wonderful. Also, toys that you throw and toys you can cuddle.

Please could you make the toys from wood, paper, cardboard and material. Rupert will give you more details.

Best wishes,

Mr Toby (Owner)

Figure 8.2

Introducing Tonica's toy workshop

Teacher's intentions

- To introduce the context for the drama;
- To introduce the teacher role of Tonica.

Discussion and improvisation: what do we know about toys?

Lead a discussion about toys. Ask children to discuss favourite toys with a partner. Share ideas.

- *What are your favourite toys?*
- *Where do we buy toys?*
- *When do we have toys as presents?*
- *What would be your favourite present?*

Ask the children to choose which toy they would like to pretend be in a toyshop. Alternatively, they could all practise being the same toy at the same time. Consider carefully how the toy 'moves'. Tell them that you will count to three, then clap your hands and they will all stand completely still (like statues) to show what toy they are. After another count of three clap hands again and the toys can come to life and move around the space. Clap again to stop. Ask children to choose a different toy.

 Descriptions, giving reasons

What's in the workshop?

Teacher's intentions

- To practise physical control;
- To develop the context of the workshop.

Freeze frames and narration: creating the workshop

The children create a freeze frame showing the toys in the workshop, which is based on the warm up activity. Either ask the children to choose which toy they would like to be in the workshop or the children can all be the same toy at the same time. Tell them that you will count to three, then clap your hands and they will all stand completely still (like statues) to show what toy they are.

While they are in the freeze frame, narrate:

Here is the workshop where I make all the toys. Here are the spinning-tops, here are the racing cars and here are the soft toys. These are some of the best-selling toys I make. We have a great demand for these at Christmas. The children love them. Do you know something secret? At night when the lights are out in the shop the toys come to life. Shall we see what they do?

Game: secrets of the workshop

(This game resembles musical statues, played with music or lights to indicate action and freeze.)

If possible, turn out the lights in the room. When the lights are out the children can move around the room as the toys. When you turn the lights on again they must return quickly to their places and become completely still, because someone may be coming. No one must know that the toys come to life! When they have returned to their places, they can begin to move about again when the lights go off and they think the coast is clear. Music from *The Nutcracker Suite* by Tchaikovsky could also be played during this activity. The music being suddenly turned off could replace the turning on and off of lights as the cue for the toys to return to their original places. Alternatively, handclaps can be the signal to move and stop.

Storytelling: setting the scene

Tell the children that you are going to tell a story about the toyshop. Start by telling the story and encourage the children to add detail.

Once there was a toymaker who loved to make toys for children. She had a workshop where she made all the toys and a small shop where people came to buy them. She made some wonderful toys. She made ... and ... [children supply ideas]. *Her toys were so popular that one day she decided that she needed some help. Lots of people wanted to work in the shop so she chose the best people from all over the world, the ones who knew lots about toys.*

Discuss what we know about the story so far.

Would you like to be those people who applied help Tonica the toymaker? You need to decide what country you have come from and why you want to work with Tonica. I am going to pretend to be Tonica the toymaker now. I'll walk in and start to talk to you.

Make collections of the children's favourite toys. Write captions and name labels for them

Collect and display stories about toys (e.g. *Old Bear* stories by Jane Hissey or *Dogger* by Shirley Hughes)

Teacher in role and discussion: meeting Tonica

Hello everyone. It's lovely to see you all here today. I'm very pleased that so many people who know about toys are coming to work with me. My mother taught me everything I know about making toys and I have no children of my own. I'd like you to make toys with me and then you will be able to carry on making toys in the workshop and selling them in the shop when I'm too old.

● *Will you tell me your names and what kind of toys you know most about?*

- *Which toys do you like best?*
- *What are you good at making?*
- *Do you know what materials you will need to make that?*
- *Would you like to look around the workshop?*

Take children on a walk around the space 'the workshop', pointing out different areas

- *This is the work bench where I keep my tools.*
- *This is where I do the glueing.*
- *I paint the toys here ...*

Out of role, discuss what has happened so far.

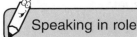 Speaking in role

Write a letter of application for the job in the toyshop

Meeting Charlie Bear

Teacher's intentions

- To develop empathy;
- To be aware of the effect of different voices;
- To engender a caring attitude.

Teacher in role: introducing a problem

Teacher in role as Tonica talks to the group:

Before we start making any new toys, we have lots of old ones that have been sent here to be mended. We'd better start on those. Oh yes, I have a bit of a problem that you might be able to help me with. Charlie Bear was brought in yesterday. He looks very sad and I haven't been able to get him to talk to me. I wonder if you could have a chat with him and find out what's wrong?

Ask the children to think of the best way to coax Charlie Bear into talking to them.

The children suggest questions that could be asked. Practise asking questions. Focus on how the question is asked.

- *Should we shout at Charlie Bear if he is silent?*
- *What kind of voice might make him feel safe with us?*
- *Let's practise using a soft voice so we don't frighten him.*

Tell the children you are going to be Charlie Bear in the next part of the story.

 Framing questions, consider register and tone appropriate to the context

Hot seating: what's wrong with Charlie Bear?

The children meet the teacher in role as Charlie Bear. They try to persuade him to talk. He is eventually coaxed to trust them and he gives the following information in response to their questions:

- *I'm a very old bear.*
- *I'm a bit tatty now as I've been hugged and cuddled so much.*
- *My squeaker doesn't work anymore.*
- *My ear is torn and my button eye is loose.*
- *My owner has just had a birthday and had loads of new toys so I've now been put on a shelf and am covered in dust.*
- *If you mend me, I may be allowed to sit on the end of his bed again.*

The children decide what could be done to cheer him up. Ask each child to suggest ways of making Charlie Bear feel better.

- *I'll brush him.*
- *I'll give him a cuddle.*
- *He could stay here with us.*
- *I'll sew his ear back on.*
- *I'll give him a new squeaker.*
- *I'll tell him a joke.*
- *It doesn't matter about the new toys. You're still special.*

Narrate what happens to Charlie Bear, depending on what the children have suggested. Perhaps he is mended and returns home, or maybe he stays at the workshop with the other toys.

 Sensitive questioning, making suggestions

Make a large group drawing of Charlie Bear and label it

A new challenge for the toymakers

Teacher's intentions

- To set a new challenge;
- To develop imagination about toy ideas and designs.

Teacher in role: Rupert's challenge

Tell the children that Tonica the toymaker has gone on holiday and they are all in charge. While she is away, a visitor arrives at the workshop. Tell the children that you will take the role of the visitor:

Hello everyone. My name's Rupert. I work for a very large toy shop in the city. I've brought a letter from my boss. Shall I read it to you? Read the letter (Figure 8.2 p. 60). As you can see, we are looking for people to make some toys for us for Christmas. We don't want electronic toys or those needing batteries as we have enough of those already. We want old-fashioned, traditional toys made of wood and cloth and card. Would you be able to design and make some toys like this for us to sell? What do you think?

Discuss possibilities. Ask the children to show you around. Suggest they start making things as soon as possible.

 Listening and responding to the teacher in role

Dramatic play: making new toys

The children get busy in the workshop, designing and making toys for Rupert through mimed activity. Props are not required. Rupert chats and makes suggestions while they work, reminding them about what he needs and what materials they can use.

 Talking in role

Draw a design of the toy and annotate it

Meeting: will the toymakers impress Rupert?

Teacher in role as Rupert invites the apprentices to gather together to show him the (imaginary) toys they have made.

- *Could you show me what you have designed/made for me?*
- *Hold it up so we can all see.*
- *What have you made? What tools did you use?*
- *Why will this be a good toy for children to have?*

Finally, he thanks them and tells them that he will write when Tonica returns to tell her how good they all are.

 Descriptive language

Put pictures of newly designed toys into a catalogue. Label the toys. Give them names and write a description to inform purchasers

Reflection: what have we learned?

Discuss how the children helped the people they met in the drama.

- *Why did Tonica need their help?*
- *Why was Charlie Bear so sad?*
- *What advice did you offer him?*
- *How did you encourage him to talk to you when he was so shy?*
- *How did you help Rupert?*
- *Why do you think they didn't want any more electronic toys?*
- *What would be your favourite toy?*

 Explain and give reasons for opinions

Use construction kits to make toys following written instructions

Chapter 9
Humpty Dumpty

Everyone enjoys this nursery rhyme, chanting it with claps and movements. But when the children meet Humpty Dumpty they are surprised to find that he sits on the wall because he is fed up. Other children don't want to play with him because he is different. He can't help being an egg. He was born this way. His mother says he should be proud to be an egg, like his parents and grandparents before him. He finds it difficult to be glad to be an egg, however, especially when it means that the children laugh at him and exclude him from their games.

Learning objectives

- To encourage a celebration of difference;
- To develop empathy;
- To practise coordination and a sense of rhythm.

Themes

- Prejudice
- Considering the feelings of others
- Nursery rhymes.

Time

- One hour.

Resources

- Humpty Dumpty rhyme

Humpty Dumpty
sat on a wall.
Humpty Dumpty
had a great fall.
All the king's horses
and all the king's men
couldn't put Humpty together again!

Delivering the rhyme

Teacher's intentions

- To develop a sense of rhythm;
- To encourage physical coordination.

Speaking together: learning the rhyme

Say the rhyme to the children. Then invite them all to join in. Divide the group into two: half say the first two lines and half say the second two lines about the king's horses and men.

Clapping with the rhyme: building up rhythm and coordination

1 Clap with every beat, i.e. on 'Hump' and 'Dump' ... ' all', 'horses'.
2 Clap on both thighs rather than hands together. Keep to every beat.
3 Try clapping with hands for the first two lines and then moving to the thighs for lines three and four.
4 With older or particularly well-coordinated children, try moving from handclaps to thigh claps alternatively.
5 This could be developed into a range of different ways of marking the beat (e.g. clap hands on head with every 'Hump' and 'Dump', or stamp feet during the king's horses lines three and four). The children can make suggestions.

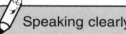 Speaking clearly and using appropriate intonation

Discuss and chant other nursery rhymes

Making gestures: adding actions to the rhyme

Discuss what action could be made for the first line. It may be a rounding gesture with both hands to indicate the shape of Humpty Dumpty, or it could focus on him sitting on a wall, or perhaps both. Practise saying the line together with the action.

Do the same for each of the four lines and say them together in a large circle so that the whole rhyme is recited with actions for each line. Discuss the sort of voice needed for each line.

 Using appropriate intonation to match action

Talking to Humpty Dumpty

Teacher's intentions

- To listen to someone's thoughts and feelings;
- To develop empathy;
- To consider difference.

Hot seating: why does Humpty sit on a wall?

Ask the children why they think Humpty might have been sitting on the wall which, after all, seems a pretty dangerous place to sit! Discuss any ideas and then explain that they can meet Humpty while he is still on the wall to try to find out. Consider how the conversation might be started.

Teacher in role as Humpty sits on a chair or box to indicate the wall and looks sad and dejected. The children sit in a group in front of Humpty and ask him why he sits there. Humpty may take a while to feel able to speak to the children. This makes the children work hard to find the right voice and questions to reassure Humpty that they are interested. The information should not be given quickly. The children find out that Humpty feels rejected by other children who don't want to play with him because he is different. He can't help being an egg. He was born this way. His mother says he should be proud to be an egg, like his parents and grandparents before him. He finds it difficult to be glad to be an egg, however, especially when it means that the children laugh at him and exclude him from their games. So he doesn't care if he falls off the wall.

Examples of Humpty's responses are:

- *You can't really be interested in talking to me.*
- *Why don't you talk to the other children over there?*
- *Everyone loves to talk and play with them.*
- *Are you really interested in talking to me? No one usually is.*
- *I wanted to join in their games, but they won't let me.*
- *They laugh at me. They call me 'scrambled' or 'poached'.*
- *I know when they laugh* with *people and when laugh* at *people. Do you know what I mean?*
- *My parents say I should be proud of who I am, but it's not very easy.*
- *My grandma says others should be happy to have friends who aren't all boringly the same. She says she has all sorts of friends. But Grandma doesn't know the children at my school.*
- *What would you say/do?*

Humpty also shares a secret. He knows that he can roll down hills faster than any of the others and is dying to see if another child could hang on to his feet and roll around fast with him. He knows the children like speed and thinks he could help them get a great ride down the hill. He'd like to do this, but doesn't wish to try while people are not nice to him.

 Selecting appropriate tone of voice and vocabulary

Speaking alternative verses. Look at different versions of Humpty Dumpty. Ask children if they know any alternative versions, such as 'Humpty Dumpty sat on a wall, eating green bananas. Where do you think he put the skin? Down the King's pyjamas!' There is a selection of alternative versions in *The Puffin Book of Nursery Rhymes* by Iona and Peter Opie. Children always enjoy listening to the German version in this book.

Addressing the problem

Teacher's intentions

- To develop the skills required to argue a moral case;
- To encourage children to stick to what is right despite pressure to do otherwise.

Group meeting and teacher in role: will the children be nice?

Invite comments about what the children think about Humpty's predicament. What would they like to say to the other children? Tell them that it may be a bit frightening to speak to crowds of children, but you can arrange for them to speak to one of the children so they can explain what they think and what Humpty thinks.

Teacher takes the role of a belligerent child who doesn't seem to care what Humpty thinks. He or she doesn't want to play with a stupid egg anyway! The children have the task of trying to change the child's attitude. You will need to vary your role depending on how forceful the children are. You may hold out for a while and say nasty things about Humpty if they seem strong enough to argue with you. Alternatively, you may need to be prepared to show that you might be wrong earlier in the conversation. You might concede that he plays marbles pretty well, for example, or that you wouldn't like it if no one played with you. They may or may not mention the hill ride that Humpty has in mind.

Ideally, the children bring the child around to a more sensitive, unprejudiced position, and they may suggest that he or she goes to speak to Humpty. But the child should not change if the children fail to persuade him or her.

 Thinking about the needs of the listener

Drawings of Humpty Dumpty. Look at the different ways that Humpty Dumpty is presented in books or children's items, such as place mats. Ask the children how they imagine him to look. Is he wearing a hat? Does he look happy or sad? Are we supposed to like him, smile about him or feel sorry for him? Individual or groups can make drawings of Humpty Dumpty.

Researching websites. There are many websites with nursery rhymes

Shared writing. The teacher leads shared writing of a unique verse of Humpty Dumpty which the children create. The emphasis is on generating a rhyme. Starter lines could be: 'Humpty Dumpty went to bed Slipped and fell and broke his ——,' or 'Humpty Dumpty sat in a tree His mother brought him a cup of ——.'

Discussion: do we tell Humpty?

Invite the children to decide whether to talk to Humpty Dumpty to tell them about the conversation they have just had. It may depend on what was said. If they wish to explain, take the role of Humpty. He might be prepared to be helped off the wall.

Class letter writing. Write a shared letter to the children to explain to them how Humpty feels. Letters could also be written from Humpty himself, or from the children to Humpty once they understand the issues. The teacher may be doing the writing on a whiteboard.

Reflection: what have we learned?

- *Why did Humpty feel different?*
- *Why didn't the children want to play with him?*
- *If there were lots of other eggs in the playground, would it have made it easier for Humpty?*
- *Would the other children have played with the eggs if there were lots of eggs?*
- *What could we say to Humpty to make him feel happier?*
- *What could we say to Humpty to make him feel stronger?*
- *What might Humpty be able to do well because he is an egg? (e.g. roll down a hill faster than any of the others).*

These are, of course, very difficult questions with no simple answers. The drama and the questions obviously concern wider issues of prejudice that disadvantages children both in and out of school.

Children can tell the story of their drama round the circle.

Explaining and giving reasons for actions

Investigate eggs. Look at different eggs on the web. Where do they come from? Look at the shells and describe it – colour, shape, texture

Chapter 10
Jack and the Beanstalk

When Jack's mother finds they have no money left for food, she has no choice but to ask Jack to sell their cow. He must get as much as he can for it because they desperately need the money. Jack faces a dilemma when he is offered magic beans rather than money for the cow. Perhaps the beans will bring good luck. Although he knows how desperate his mother is for money for food this very day, he decides to take the beans. When the beanstalk grows, Jack climbs up to see the giant sleeping beside a pile of golden eggs. His attempt to creep up and retrieve the eggs fails when the giant wakes and booms that the boy is a wicked thief. He asks the children what he should do with Jack. How should the giant punish Jack for trying to steal?

Learning objectives

- To develop children's understanding of the importance of tone and expression for communicating meaning and emotion;
- To encourage creativity in making up story endings;
- To invite group shared responsibility.

Themes

- Fairytales
- Stealing – moral dilemmas.

Resources – optional

- A few beans, such as broad beans, jellybeans or even buttons or coins;
- Props to represent golden eggs or gold coins;
- Real beans/bulbs/seeds or avocado pear stones for planting.

Time

- Ninety minutes.

Notes

In this drama the children explore nuances of language in a very simple way. They say lines in different ways and with different gestures so that the meanings change. It can easily be related to everyday class speech in which gesture, tone and facial expression are often more significant to meaning than the words. 'I didn't do it,' for example, can be said with many different overtones!

Figure 10.1 An imaginative play area in the Giant's Castle

The cow must be sold

Teacher's intentions

- To introduce the story;
- To consider the way we understand language through more than the words;
- To experiment ways of changing meaning with tone of voice and gesture.

Narration: the story begins

The familiar story is told up to the moment Jack is sent on his way to sell the cow. They are desperate for money for food. The last thing that Jack's mother says to him is, 'Get lots of money for food, Jack!'

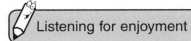
Listening for enjoyment

Read different versions of the well known fairytale or talk about pictures from different story books

Whole-group line delivery: emphasizing meaning through voice and gesture

Discuss and try out with the children how certain lines would have been delivered.

● *How might she have said 'Get lots of money for food, Jack!' to show she is desperate?*

Make a hand gesture to indicate when to say the line all together. Try the line at different volumes by moving your arm up for loud and down for soft.

● *What gesture may she have used?*

All try pointing a finger with the line.

● *What do we understand by this?* (Giving clear instruction to Jack.)

All try holding up hands against her head. (She is desperate for Jack to get this right.) Try these lines loudly and softly and see what difference it makes.
  Some children may wish to deliver the line with a gesture of their own. They are encouraged to see how the same lines can communicate different meanings. How about:

● As if she is weak with hunger (and the gestures?);
● As if she is a very strong and powerful woman;
● As if she is always nagging Jack.

Expressing feelings

Consideration of volume, gesture and underlying meanings

Narration: Jack sells the cow

Jack walks towards market with the cow. He is getting tired when he meets a strange old woman. She offers him magic beans instead of money for the cow. He explains that he needs money, but she says,
  'Take these magic beans, my boy.'

Whole-group line delivery: what would the strange woman mean?

● *How might she have said the words 'Take these magic beans, my boy' to show she is desperate? What gesture may she have used?*
● *What if she wanted Jack to know that the beans were magic?*
● *What if she meant to frighten Jack into taking the beans?*
● *What if she wanted to be very kind to Jack?*

Again, the class can chant the lines together in different ways with different gestures.

Listening and responding

Speaking with appropriate intonation

Experimenting with voice and gesture

Jack's decision to take the beans

Teacher's intentions

- To develop vocal control and a sense of timing;
- To practise concentration when responding to a cue;
- To consider choices.

Chorus work: focus on voice, gesture and body language

Divide the class into two halves with each half at either end of the room. One half represents Jack's mother and says her line *(Get lots of money for food, Jack!)* and the other, the strange old lady *(Take these magic beans, my boy).* Agree with each side how they want to say their line, using ideas from the voice experiments above. They consider the voice and gesture.

Teacher in role as Jack stands in the middle of the room holding the beans in his hands. He is wondering what to do. When he looks towards the old lady, the children must all repeat her line until the moment he turns away. Then they fall silent. When Jack looks at his mother's group, they repeat her line until he looks away again. He should turn to each a few times as he tries to decide what to do.

Jack will look down at some point, so all the children will be silent then. He may toy with the beans and may add some words in between, such as:

- *Perhaps something good will come of the beans.*
- *My mother is so hungry. I shouldn't do this.*

This activity is about verbal expression, coordination and the concentration to respond at the appropriate time. It is fun to do, and it highlights Jack's dilemma. Finally, he makes the decision: 'Have our cow. I will take your beans!'

Speaking with emphasis and emotion

See versions of the story on websites

Read other 'Jack' stories, e.g. a sequel, *Jim and the Beanstalk* by Raymond Briggs, and *Jack and the Three Sillies* by Richard Chase, a humorous American version of a Jack from England.

The beans could be magic

Teacher's intentions

- To provide an opportunity for a contribution from each child in a safe context
- To stretch the imagination in search of different possibilities

Conscience alley: has Jack been a fool?

The children form two winding lines facing each other to create the path Jack followed on his way home. The teacher or a child holds the beans and very slowly wanders down the path (e.g. between the two lines of children). As Jack passes each child, he or she says how he or she thinks the beans might be magic or what they might grow into.

- *They may turn into gold.*
- *They could grow into a beanstalk.*
- *They will make him rich.*
- *They aren't magic at all.*
- *They may provide beans to eat forever.*

 Prediction and use of appropriate tone of voice

Hypothesis: look at a range of beans, bulbs and seeds and discuss what they might grow into. Drawings with notes of colour, texture and size before they are planted are compared with drawing made once they have grown

Statementing: what might Jack's mother say?

- What might Jack's mother have said when Jack came home with the beans?

Children make a few suggestions and share ideas of gestures that might help to make the meaning clear.

- Was she angry? Upset? Desperate? Crazy?

Stand in the middle of a circle of children. The teacher, in role as Jack holding out the beans, will approach a child. The child gives a response that his mother might give. Jack can react and then move on to another child in the circle. The mother's lines might include:

- *Go to your bed at once!*
- *What will we do for food now?*
- *How can you be so stupid?*

>
> Responding to the story

> Listening to stories recorded by actors provides a way to listen to different expression. How different are the giants' voices? Which sound most frightening?
>
> The imaginative play area can be designed as the Giant's castle

Climbing the beanstalk

Teacher's intentions

- To move the story on;
- To use physical activity to tell the story.

Narration and mimed action: magic happens!

The next part of the story is told in as much detail as you wish:

Jack sleeps well, but perhaps his mother does not sleep so well! In the morning Jack sees the huge beanstalk. When he looks up he realizes it goes up and up as far as he can see. He decides to climb it.

Invite the children to imagine climbing the beanstalk pretending to be Jack. Lead the children in mimed action through describing climbing the beanstalk and demonstrating the gestures.

You can use this activity to teach left and right as you refer to reaching with your right or left arm with a large arm movement e.g.

'He first put his right hand up to the highest branch he could reach. Then he pulled himself up by placing his left foot on a lower branch. Slowly he raised his right foot, but ... he slipped and nearly fell. Luckily his right hand was strong enough to hang on.'

>
> Listening to the story
>
> Listening and responding to what is said

> List words to describe the beanstalk

Figure 10.2 Jack climbs the beanstalk by Charlie

Creeping up on the giant

Teacher's intentions

- To provide the opportunity to develop physical agility and control;
- To consider the consequences of Jack's actions;
- To introduce ethical questions about wealth.

Game: keeping quite matters

Play Keeper of the keys (see Games on page xvi). This game encourages physical control and dexterity. Here it is a way of working towards the dramatic moment when Jack tries to steal from the giant, below. Also play Grandmother's footsteps in preparation for creeping up on the giant.

Storytelling: Jack creeps in to the giant's home

The children are invited to fill the gaps in this narration so that together they will build up a picture of the giant's room.

When Jack eventually reached the top of the beanstalk he found himself in a huge room, with huge furniture and huge walls, doors and ceilings. There was also a huge ... and a massive ... He saw the most enormous ... a gigantic ... and a giant-sized ...

Under the chair that was as big as a... Jack saw some golden eggs. The giant was sound asleep, so Jack wondered if he could creep over and reach under the giant's chair and get hold of some of those eggs. If he got even one egg, he and his mother would never be hungry again.

 Speaking in turn; listening and responding

Whole-class improvisation/game and discussion: is Jack a thief?

Take the role of the giant and sit in a chair snoring. The children sit in a large circle around you and use the action as in the game 'Keeper of the Keys' (see 'Games' p. xvi). Place something under the chair to represent the golden eggs. The children try to creep slowly nearer to the chair with the aim to get the eggs. However, every time they get somewhere near, the giant moves, grunts or twitches, which sends them back to the edge where they can't be seen.

When a child reaches out to get the eggs, the giant touches him – *Got you!* – then jumps up on to a chair and says in a big, deep voice:

This boy is a thief! This boy has entered my house when he wasn't invited. He didn't even ask to come in or knock on the door! He has crept up on me in my sleep and tried to steal my eggs.

I am a strong giant, but I am a fair giant. What do you think I should do with him? Shall I eat him? Shall I crush him? Should he be made to clean my house each day for five years?

Tell me, how should I punish this boy?

The children will probably explain that Jack and his mother are hungry and that he didn't mean any harm. The drama ends once the children have decided what should happen and have persuaded the giant to do this. Many want the giant and Jack to be friends and for the giant to let Jack have just one egg. The giant may insist on an apology. The giant may decide it is wrong for him to have so much and not even use it, when others like Jack's family are starving. It may turn out that the giant had worked for his wealth, or had stolen it himself. Perhaps, long ago, he had plundered the village at the foot of the beanstalk!

Whatever the children decide can be discussed and acted out.

 Show understanding of stories

Speaking clearly to give ideas

Reflection: what have we learned?

Discussion can be about who was right and who was wrong in this story.

Consider lines we might use in everyday life and consider the different ways they could be said and which ways are more appropriate in different contexts. An example is,' All right. You can borrow my ruler.' Try saying it:

- with affection
- to tease
- as if you do not want to lend it
- to upset the borrower.

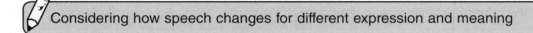 Considering how speech changes for different expression and meaning

Make a big book with words from the story

Chapter 11
Cinderella

Ella, or Cinderella as her two nasty sisters call her, is a rather sad and weak girl. The children meet her and are able to give her advice about dealing with and standing up to her bullying sisters. When an invitation arrives inviting all the girls to the Prince's birthday party at the palace, her two sisters tell Ella that she can't go, as there is too much work to do at home. Ella does go to the party, but in this version of the story it is not because of a fairy godmother. Ella's friends help to give her confidence and show her useful strategies for increasing her self-esteem. She manages to persuade her sisters to allow her to go to the party, where she decides whether or not to marry the Prince.

Learning objectives

● To explore bullying;
● To practise assertive and persuasive language.

Themes

● Fairytales
● Bullying
● Sibling rivalry.

Time

● Two hours.

Resources – optional

● Large sheet of paper and felt-tip pens;
● apron for Cinderella;
● hat or shawl for sisters.

Notes

The imaginative play area can be designed as a kitchen, a palace ballroom or a castle. This drama takes a twist on the traditional Cinderella story. It is useful but not essential that the children have heard the traditional version before doing the drama, but not immediately before the lesson. The traditional story introduces Cinderella's sisters as stepsisters and the mother is a stepmother. You might prefer to leave this out. The drama will explore the issue of sibling rivalry, but does not set out to deal with issues of reconstituted families unless this comes directly from the children. It is important that you make it clear to the children that this version of the story is different from ones they may have seen (Disney) and there are no talking animals in this version!

What is the matter with the girl?

Teacher's intentions

- To use mime as an introduction;
- To introduce the teacher in role as Cinderella;
- To focus on body language and facial expression.

Mime: what can we tell about this person by watching a mime?

Tell the children that they are going to watch you doing a mime. You are Cinderella but don't tell the children! Include some of the following: pretend to pick up a broom and begin to sweep the floor. Pretend to polish, dust clean. Carry a heavy bucket of coal. Wipe your forehead. Sigh. Look downcast and unhappy. Rub your hands near the fire to warm them. Sit down close to the fire and go to sleep. Talk to the children about who you were and what you were doing.

- *What did they see?*
- *What was the person doing?*
- *Who was the person in the mime?*
- *How was the person feeling?*
- *How do we know?*

The children may instantly recognise who it is but try to draw out how we know she is feeling sad. Focus on the body language and facial expressions.

> Happy and sad words collected and displayed on a happy and sad faces
>
> Collect different versions of the story

Hot seating: meeting Cinderella

Tell the children that they will be able to talk to Ella. How will they approach a sad girl? What do they want to find out? Frame some questions together. Information is given by the teacher in role. Feel free to give as much detail as you like, such as:

- *My name is Ella but everyone calls me Cinderella because I usually fall asleep in the hearth by the fire, in among the cinders. That's why my sisters call me Cinderella.*

- *I don't mind because it's lovely and warm there.*
- *I'm so tired because I do all the work in the house.*
- *My mother and sisters are rather lazy but I don't mind doing the work. It's fun really.*

 Asking questions, choosing appropriate tone and register for talk

Role on the wall: what do we know about Ella?

Draw an outline of Cinderella. Recap on what has been learned about Cinderella. The information is jotted around the figure. Feelings expressed by Ella or identified by the children can be written inside the figure.

This could also be done for the two sisters, focusing on adjectives to describe them. The role on the wall can be added to when more information is known. It helps with recapping the plot and also recording the feelings of different characters.

 Using adjectives to describe, summarizing information

The story begins

Teacher's intentions

- To retell part of the story of Cinderella;
- To focus on the characters of the sisters;
- To use thought tapping.

Storytelling, mime and thought tapping

Recap the different characteristics of Cinderella and her sisters. Ask the children to mime the first part of the story of Cinderella as you tell it. They will do this individually so will be in role as all the different characters as they appear in the story. Your story should be descriptive enough to enable them to portray easily the differences in the characters and should use some of the children's words which were given in the previous activity.

Once there was a girl called Cinderella. She worked very hard all day long in the kitchen, sweeping the floor, washing the dishes, polishing the ornaments, putting coal on the fire ... (Use ideas from the hot seating activity.)

Ask the children to freeze and then thought tap a few of them.

- *How do you feel about doing all the work in the house?*
- *Don't you think your sisters should do more to help?*
- *Why do they make you do everything?*

Tell the children they will now be portraying the sisters and then continue with the story:

Cinderella's sisters were older than her and not very nice. One was tall and looked angry all the time. She stamped around the house, shaking her fist at Cinderella. The other was short with rounded shoulders. She always frowned and never smiled. She always shook her head at Cinderella and wagged her finger at her to make her work harder.

Ask the children to freeze, and again thought tap them, this time as the sisters.

- *Why don't you ever help Cinderella to do the work?*
- *Why are you so unkind to her?*

Listening and interpretation of instructions

Record the thoughts of the characters in thought bubbles or add thought bubbles to the role on the wall picture created earlier

Write descriptions of each of the main characters

Freeze frames and thought tapping: scenes between the sisters

Ask children to work in groups of three (or four). One child is in role as Ella, two as the sisters, and possibly the mother if working in groups of four. Roles can be allocated or children choose themselves. Ask them to prepare a scene where the characters are interacting. Freeze the scenes one at a time and thought tap the roles.

Working in role, devising scenes, rehearsing and performing

Look at script writing. Investigate layout and stage directions

An invitation arrives

Teacher's intentions

- To work in groups to present a scene;
- To consider aspects of theatre skills – voice, space, awareness of audience.

Storytelling and improvisation

Children are still working in groups from previous activity. Continue telling more of the story while the groups act it out. You can put in different events to allow children to deepen commitment to their new roles.

If the sisters ever needed anything, they would always call Cinderella – 'I'm hungry, get me some food!'
'I'm thirsty, get me a drink!'

Continue this as long as the children are engaged.
Ask the groups to sit down and listen to the next part of the story.

One day an invitation arrived from the palace. The Prince was having a party to celebrate his birthday and was inviting all the girls in the land. You see, he wanted to find a girl to marry! Cinderella and her sisters looked at the invitation excitedly. But then the sisters said to Cinderella, 'Well, don't get so excited, Cinderella. You are not going. The Prince would not want a dirty girl like you there. He wants to marry a beautiful girl, like us.'

Ask the groups to practise acting out this scene. They can add other words. Discuss some of the acting skills necessary to think about – voice, space and audience. Success criteria for the performances can be agreed. The scene should end with a freeze frame showing the feelings of each character clearly.

Give groups time to rehearse and then show each other their scenes. Talk about the 'performances'. Ask other groups to give positive feedback about what they liked and also suggest ways of improving the work.

Speaking in role; taking in to account the needs of listeners; commenting constructively on drama they have watched

Video the scenes and look at them closely with regard to the agreed specific success criteria

Write invitations to the party

Design a webpage for the Prince

What can Cinderella do?

Teacher's intentions

- To encourage the children to offer ways for Cinderella to stand up to her sisters;
- To reflect on people who are bullies and what should be done about them;
- To practise using voice, body language and a reasoned argument to express a point of view;
- To work in groups to solve problems.

Thought tracking: how is Cinderella feeling?

Ask the children to sit in a circle. Discuss:

- *What does Cinderella want to do?*
- *Why won't her sisters let her go to the party?*
- *Why are they treating her like this?*

You can put a chair in the middle to represent Cinderella or you could sit on the chair in role. Ask the children to imagine what Cinderella is feeling at this point in the story.

Ask them to speak aloud her thoughts one at a time around the circle.

- *I feel sad.*
- *I want to go to the party.*
- *They can't stop me.*
- *I think they're mean and horrid.*

Discussion and teacher in role: advising Cinderella

Tell the children that in some stories there is a fairy godmother who makes things work out well for Cinderella. However, in this story there is no fairy godmother to make it all right! If Cinderella wants to go to the party she must think of how to stand up to her sisters and persuade them to let her go. Ask them to discuss the ideas in small groups. Share their ideas.

Tell the children that you are going to be in role as Ella and they are going to tell you their ideas about how to persuade the sisters. Be quiet, shy and reluctant to be assertive. Ask the children to show you how to act. Remember that assertive doesn't mean aggressive, but it is important to get over your point of view calmly! The focus is on tone, volume, body language and use of persuasive language.

- *I couldn't ask my sisters if I can go. I'm too nervous.*
- *What shall I say?*
- *How should I say it?*
- *Like this?* [Shouting] *That's no good, they'll shout back.*

Try to encourage suggestions about what could really be said to bullies to make them stop, e.g. telling someone else about the problem (father/mother/the Prince?). The children prepare the teacher in role to solve her own problem.

Children could be asked to demonstrate how to say things in appropriate ways as a 'model' for Cinderella. Finally, out of role, narrate:

So Cinderella took the children's advice and went to speak to her sisters.

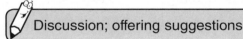 Discussion; offering suggestions

Write advice on a Post-it note and stick on the role on the wall created earlier

Small group improvisation: facing up to the sisters

Ask children to work in original small groups. They should start with the freeze frame they finished with in the previous activity then start the improvisation again to see how the Cinderella in each group uses the advice she has been given to stand up to the sisters. These improvisations can be rehearsed a couple of times and then watched if appropriate.

Using persuasive language in role; developing an argument

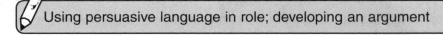 Improvisations can be filmed, played back and discussed

The party

Teacher's intentions

- To give feedback to the children;
- To enable the children to evaluate the effectiveness of their ideas.

Teacher in role: Ella is going to the party!

Tell the children that Cinderella stood up for herself and is now able to go to the party. She is now coming to tell them about it: Encourage children to add ideas.

[Excitedly] *Well, you'll never guess! I said exactly what you told me about ...* [Use ideas the children suggested] *and they said I could go. They weren't very happy about it. They took some persuading, but they said I was right. The only problem is that I have nothing to wear! What should I wear to a party at the palace? A dress? Silver slippers? Oh I could never buy any of those things. I haven't got much money.*

Take children's suggestions (e.g. borrow a dress, alter an old one – they may offer to give you one or make one). Ask them to describe how you will look in your new dress.

> Describing; making suggestions

> Plan the party
>
> Discuss how the room would be set out. What food, drink and music would there be?
>
> Draw and annotate a design for a dress for Cinderella
>
> Watch sections of the Disney cartoon version of *Cinderella*

Thought tunnel: how does Ella feel about going to the party?

Discuss how Cinderella is feeling now – happy, nervous, excited, and can't wait to get there?
Children stand in two lines facing each other. Teacher in role as Cinderella walks along the path to the party. Children speak her thoughts as she passes them.

- *I'm really scared about meeting the Prince.*
- *I want to dance!*
- *I'm excited!*
- *What will there be to eat?*

Freeze frame and whole group improvisation: at the party

You may decide to allocate specific roles to children for this activity: King, Queen, Prince, sisters, guests. Discuss what would happen at the party (e.g. drinking, chatting, dancing, playing games, eating). Ask the children to set up the party scene. This could be done as a freeze frame which is brought to life. Teacher in role as Cinderella enters the scene and walks around meeting people. This activity can go on for as long as you want, depending on the involvement of the children.

How did the party end? The children may choose the traditional ending or suggest an alternative. The children must decide whether or not Ella chooses to marry the Prince. Each child can say *Yes* or *No* and could provide a reason.

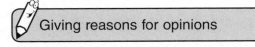
Giving reasons for opinions

Write the end of the story

Write a newspaper report or an engagement announcement

Reflection: what have we learned?

Talk about the situation of Cinderella and her sisters.

- *How did Cinderella change things?*
- *How did she need to change?*
- *How should the sisters change?*

Revisit the roles on the way and see whether any of the characteristics attributed earlier can be changed.

Discuss what to do if someone is mean to them. Discuss the importance of telling someone about a problem and the importance of friends to give advice and support.

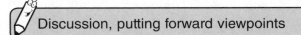
Discussion, putting forward viewpoints

Tell or read the story of Cinderella

Tell the story from the viewpoint of one of the characters

Figure 11.1 Ugly sisters by Beth

Chapter 12
Suzie and the Snow

Suzie is sad and won't go out to play in the snow. The children try to find out why and gradually learn about Suzie's accident on the ice last year. The past is brought to life with the children all taking part in it. Finally, they advise her about how she can play out in the snow safely.

Learning objectives

- To know about keeping safe in the snow;
- To be able to use appropriate language in a sensitive situation;
- To develop empathy.

Themes

- Safety
- Caring for others
- Citizenship
- Friendship.

Resources

- Suzie's diary entry is provided (see Figure 12.1);
- A jacket.

Time

- Approximately one hour or longer if the work is videoed in the final activity.

What is the matter with Suzie?

Teacher's intentions

- To introduce the story;
- To encourage children to interact with the teacher in role sensitively and ask questions to discover the problem.

Discussion: what do we know about diaries?

Sit in a circle. Explain that you will be doing a drama about an imaginary little girl called Suzie. You will pretend to have a page from her diary (see Figure 12.1).

- *What is a diary?*
- *Why might some diaries be secret?*
- *Who uses diaries?*
- *What is put into diaries?*

Read the diary provided to the children. Ask the class to listen to the diary and try to work out what is going on. Discuss.

- *Which single words would describe how she feels?*
- *Why is she feeling like this, do you think?*
- *Why doesn't she like the snow?*
- *What might have happened?*
- *What could her Dad have meant by saying she could play sensibly?*

Comprehension; prediction; vocabulary extension

Draw large, sad face. List words appropriate to the sad face and Suzie, e.g. sad, lost, scared

Read books written in diary format e.g. *Diary of a Wombat* by Jackie French

Meeting Suzie

Teacher's intentions

- To introduce the teacher in role;
- To talk to the teacher in role;
- To discover the problem.

Teacher in role and questioning

Invite the class to meet Suzie to try to find out what has happened.

- *What should they ask?*
- *How should they speak to someone who is upset?*
- *What should they begin with saying?*
- *How will they ensure Suzie knows that she can trust them?*
- *What sort of voices and expression should they use?*
- *What does a 'kind' voice (or any other suggestion) sound like?*

Teacher leaves the circle and returns as Suzie. She is very, very shy and hardly dares to look at the children. She hesitates before sitting in the circle, or may even wait to be

---

FEBRUARY 16th

I heard the weather on the television. It said there may be snow. I wish it could be summer. Oh, please don't let it snow. All my friends will be out. They'll be knocking on the door. They wont understand why I wont go out with them. My Dad says I'm silly and that I could play out sensibly, though I know he stills feels afraid about what happened. My sister doesn't like being out in the snow much now either.

The weather man does get it wrong sometimes, Dad says he does. Maybe he was wrong this time.

Figure 12.1 Suzie's diary (This could be photocopied and enlarged for use with the class)

invited to sit down. Suzie could have a mannerism to depict her shyness, such as tugging on her sleeve or swinging her legs or wrapping them around the chair leg.

Suzie does not give much information away and at first changes the subject if asked about snow! She talks about Lego cranes, boats and summer games ... anything but snow and winter!

If the children do not press Suzie to talk, then entice questions by giving incomplete information

'I don't like going out – not after what happened.'

Eventually, she feels ready to tell the class:

It was a snowy Sunday ... everyone was there in the park ... fun, snowballs, sledging, scarves and woolly hats ... I boasted about my ice skating ... I said that I could skate up the river, round the three bends, through the wood to the bridge and back ... they warned me ... they all said I mustn't, said I was silly ... I wish I'd listened ...

Suzie leaves the circle, too upset to go on.

Framing questions; using appropriate register; choosing vocabulary

Teacher models asking questions, inappropriate and inappropriate tones and expressions. Children identify which are best for Suzie

Discussion

- *What did you find out?*
- *How do you think she felt?*
- *Why did she leave us?*

Last year in the park

Teacher's intentions

- To recreate the park scene with children taking roles;
- To find out what happened to Suzie in the park.

Defining space, dramatic play, freeze frames and questioning: what happened in the park?

Suggest that they all go back in time to find out what happened in the park. First, they need to create a big picture of the scene at the park that day. Everyone will become a person in that scene who was there that day.

- *What do we know about the park that day?*
- *What were you doing?*
- *Whereabouts were you?*

Define and organize the space:

- *Where shall we imagine the river is?*
- *Where is the slope for the sledging?*
- *In which direction are the woods and the bridge that Suzie spoke of?*

Children move into the space and decide who they were with and what they were doing on that day. They can improvise the scene for a few minutes before they are asked to freeze in an image depicting their activity – for example, snowballing or building a snowman. Teacher admires the scene they have created and explains that she can move into this scene and bring people to life by touching their shoulders. A second tap on their shoulders freezes them again.

Tap individuals and ask about what they are doing, who they are throwing a snowball at, what the snow feels like in the fingers, what it feels like to sledge so quickly, what will be used for the snowman's eyes, and so on. A second tap freezes them into still silence again so that the scene remains fixed.

> Descriptive language; talking in role

> Write a description of the scene in the park or draw pictures of the people and label them with their activities

Figure 12.2 A Snowman by Phoebe

Teacher in role and narration: Suzie shows off

Explain that you will take the role of Suzie. As you speak to the children they will come to life and respond. Check that they remember the sort of things that the other children had said to Suzie when she boasted about her skating idea. After you have spoken to them they become part of the still image again.

Suzie enters from one side and explains her idea to individuals and small groups of children. They will answer back, saying she is silly, or something similar. She moves on to try to persuade others to join her, calling them 'chickens' and 'cowards'. Once she has approached all the children she moves towards the edge of the area in the direction of the woods and bridge, and then turns around suddenly. Now narrate in an excited tone. (This can be read from the page if it is more comfortable for you. It doesn't spoil the effect, although just speaking the story is more fun.)

She skated up the river, got around the first two bends and was quickly in the wood. The air was crisp; the woods were quiet. Suddenly she felt a crack under her foot. She lurched forward in an attempt to keep her balance, but almost at once her right foot was through the ice.

Scrambling, gasping, panicking, soon she was in the icy cold water up to her arm-pits, arms stretched out so she wouldn't go down completely. The shouting and screaming became frantic shrieking, but no one heard. She was too far away. She couldn't feel much of her body, it all felt numb and her hands were hardly recognizable, being a blend of red and blue. She wondered how long she could keep her position. Would anyone walk far enough into the wood to see or hear her?

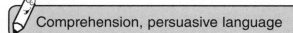
Comprehension, persuasive language

Thought tracking: Suzie's thoughts

Figure 12.3 Suzie's thoughts

The children stand in a circle. Teacher moves into the middle and places a jacket on the floor, arranging it carefully in silence, positioning the arms outstretched either side.

Stepping back into the circle, ask the children to think about what Suzie will be thinking as she clings on to the ice. One at a time children take a step forward and say something that Suzie could have been thinking (see Figure 12.3).

 Selecting appropriate language

Record Suzie's thoughts in thought bubbles on large paper

Suzie's escape

Teacher's intentions

● To consider solutions.

Story circles or puppets: telling what happened

We know that Suzie survived because we met her a year after the accident. How was she rescued? The possible stories of her rescue can be told in either of the following ways.

Story circle
Children work in the whole class group and take it in turns to tell a little bit of the story of her way out of the ice. By the time they get around the whole circle the story must finish. This means that they all need to consider how much or how little to tell when it is their turn. Story circles could also be carried out with small groups. Each group tells a story going around their circle a few times.

 Sequencing and storytelling

Matching voices to characters

Puppets
In small groups, the story is made up and then told using puppets. Puppets need not be 'real' puppets, but anything that happens to be around. We have seen pencil cases used as rescuers and plants as the crying Suzie. Each child manipulates a puppet and provides its voice, as well as some narration.

Tell or write the story of Suzie's rescue from different perspectives – her mum, a newspaper, a TV report, her friends. Groups prepare using appropriate tone to read or present.

Individual writing or shared writing task. Children write additional entries in a diary as Suzie, or as other children who were in the park

Persuading Suzie to play out

Teacher's intentions

- To provide a positive ending to the story.

Whole class meeting and teacher in role: persuading Suzie

Discuss the following questions with the children.

- *How can we help Suzie, who is* still *afraid to go out in the snow?*
- *Would we be able to explain that it can be safe to play out in the snow?*
- *Do you think you could encourage her to go outside?*
- *What would you say?*
- *Shall I get Suzie?*

The task is set: the children now try to advise Suzie that she could play out, enjoy herself and still be perfectly safe. Teacher in role as Suzie is reluctant at first, making the class work hard to convince her. Finally, when they convince her, she says she will go and get her Wellington boots.

Reflection: what have we learned?

Discuss the drama.

- *What has Suzie learned from her experience?*
- *How did we help her to overcome her fears?*
- *What have we learned about safety on the ice?*

> Create a poster to warn children of dangers on the ice. Write rules for safe behaviour
>
> Investigate: weather forecasts and symbols; living in snowy climates; travelling in snow

Safety promotion videos

Teacher's intentions

- To provide extension activity;
- To consolidate learning;
- To provide an option for ICT group activity.

Group work

This activity will be appropriate for some children who can work on their own in groups. It will obviously take a few hours if the children's work is filmed.

Speak to the children as though they are film-makers. Tell them that, as a result of Suzie's accident, all school children are to be shown a film that warns children about the dangers of snow and moving about on ice, giving advice on safety. (You may prefer to choose a local hazardous environment such as gravel pits or mudflats.) It is crucial that the films are fun and lively so that the children they are aimed at will enjoy them and take the message seriously.

In small groups the children plan and perform something that they think would be suitable for the film. They may include an interview with Suzie or a friend, they may make up a jingle, make a number of points to remember in an appropriate language register, or they may construct a re-enactment of the accident. In some schools it may be possible to film the groups' work and show the films to other classes, or in an assembly. Titles or captions can be made on large sheets of sugar paper or whiteboards and filmed with sound effects of words, noises or music.

Figure 12.4 Snowman by Beth

Chapter 13
Trouble at the Bottom of the Sea

Based on *'The Rainbow Fish'* by Marcus Pfister

Learning Objectives

- To be able to use appropriate language in a sensitive situation;
- To develop empathy.

Themes

- Friendship
- Sharing
- Envy
- Considering the feelings of others.

Suggested resources (the drama can be taught without these)

- *The Rainbow Fish* by Marcus Pfister, translated from the original Spanish by J. Alison James (North–South Books 1-55858-441-2);
- Pictures of fish and sea creatures on cards or pictures prepared to display on screen;
- Shiny material/robe for Rainbow Fish;
- Cloak or strip of shiny material for shining fish.

Time

- One hour.

Notes

It is useful to have a copy of the book and the opportunity to enlarge the pictures on screen is an advantage. This is a popular book, but it does not matter if the children are familiar with it. Some of the activities can be shortened.

Setting the scene – who are we and where are we?

Teacher's intentions

- To set the scene;
- To introduce teacher and children's roles.

Discussion and hot seating: under the sea

Tell the children that in their drama today they will be telling a story about some fish and other creatures that live under the sea in a special part of the ocean. Ask children to name types of fish and sea creatures they have heard of.

● *Has anyone visited an aquarium?*

Tell the children you are going to take on the role of the Old Grey Fish and they will be able to ask questions about what life is like in this part of the ocean. (Feel free to create a different name for your role.)

In pairs, discuss questions to ask the Old Grey Fish.

If you like, cover the teacher's chair with a shiny cloth to make it a little more special and theatrical.

Go into role by walking over to the door and returning slowly to sit back down on the hot seat. Introduce yourself:

Hello everyone, my name is Old Grey Fish. I think you might have some questions for me!

Be careful to give accurate information but also be creative by adding extra details that would not affect the story. If the children begin to make links with the *Rainbow Fish* story, try to avoid this by saying that you have heard of a fish called Rainbow Fish but you have never met him. You hear he is very beautiful. The children may try to introduce other well-known fish to this story, e.g. Nemo. This is fine. Perhaps tell them that you have heard about Nemo, but he doesn't live around here.

Tell the children about the sea creatures who are your friends e.g. octopus, squid, angel fish, crab, lobster. It is useful to have some pictures prepared, which you can show to the children, or have some prepared to display on the screen:

Here is a picture/photograph of my friend the star fish. He lives behind a big rock.

Talk about what we have learned about the ocean from the Old Grey Fish.

> Suggesting; offering ideas; sharing experiences
>
> Asking questions, remembering specific points

> Make a list of fish and sea creatures
>
> Reading – research sea creatures, print off pictures, make an under-sea collage and label it or add a caption

Collaborative storytelling: the beginning

Tell the children that you will begin to tell a story about these sea creatures. You will be asking some children to add details and ideas to the story as it goes along. They will know when to speak because you will look directly at them.

A long way out in the deep ocean, where the water is sparkling and clear, the fish and other sea creatures play all day among the weeds. There are all kinds of beautifully coloured fish. Some are red and some are ... [make eye contact with a child and encourage them to supply an appropriate word] *Others are ... and some are ... The fish play with the other sea creatures such as the octopus and the ... and the ... They play all kinds of games together such as hide and seek and ... and ... They all live very happily together in their beautiful undersea world. The fish and the sea creatures like it in their part of the ocean because it is beautiful and ... and ... Everyone is happy there.*

Choose words carefully, include relevant detail

Record the story as it is told to listen to again later

Developing a role: meeting the fishy friends

Ask the group to sit in pairs. Ask them all to think about the fish or the sea creature they would like to be in the story – give time for pairs to decide and begin to develop their own role. Ask each one to introduce themselves to the whole group or to a partner, perhaps give them a name and say where they live in the sea.

Hello, my name is Shining Fish. I am green and yellow and I like eating weeds.

Organize ideas; communicate ideas clearly

Draw a picture and write a sentence about your character

What is it like to live under the sea?

Teacher's intentions

● To work in role.

Freeze-frame and whole-group improvisation: under the sea

Tell the group that in the next activity you will pretend the classroom is the ocean and you will all be the fish and sea creatures living there. Ask them to stand or sit in a space of their own. Say that when you clap your hands they will 'freeze' as a whole group freeze frame. Say they will listen to a bit of the story and then when you clap your hands they will be the fish and the creatures in the story and can move around in the space. You will be in role as Old Grey Fish.

Narrate that it is a lovely bright morning. All the creatures are going about their business, playing or chatting with each other in the ocean. Clap your hands and start the action. In role as Old Grey Fish, move amongst the fish, chatting with them and asking questions about what they are doing.

Freeze frame and thought tap: more of life under the sea

After a few minutes, clap again and freeze the action. Talk to individuals by tapping them on the shoulder. Ask questions about their lives:

- *Who are your best friends?*
- *What do you eat?*
- *Tell me about your ...*
- *Where do you live?*

Restart the action again with a clap and repeat this two or three times until you have spoken to most of the group.

A possible problem here could be that someone mentions Rainbow Fish. The teacher in role as Old Grey Fish should accept what is said but emphasize that she has not heard or seen anything of this new fish yet.

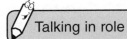 Talking in role

Speech bubbles could be added to the pictures drawn previously

There's a new fish in town

Teacher's intentions

- To introduce a new role who has a problem to solve;
- To give advice to the teacher in role.

Defining space, meeting with teacher in role: news from Old Grey Fish

Tell the group that in the next part of the story they are going to be called to a meeting by Old Grey Fish. There is something important to tell them all and to talk about.

Arrange the space for a meeting, perhaps sitting in row or a circle so all can see. Teacher in role as Old Grey Fish welcomes everyone to the meeting and asks if they are all well. He explains he has heard rumours about a new fish that has come to this part of the ocean. He has heard his name is Rainbow Fish and he has beautiful shining scales.

- *Has anyone heard anything about him or seen him?*
- *Has anyone met him?*
- *What is he like?*
- *Is he friendly?*
- *Has he been playing with them?*

Say that you have heard that Little Blue Fish has asked for one of his beautiful shining scales because they are so pretty.

- *Has anyone heard about this?*
- *Was it a good idea to ask for a scale?*
- *Have any of you tried to make friends or spoken to Rainbow Fish? Perhaps he is shy?*
- *Would you like to meet him and become friends?*
- *Do you think he should give Little Blue Fish one of his scales?*

> Take turns in speaking; listen to others' ideas and opinions

> Role on the wall: draw a big outline of Rainbow Fish. Write any thoughts about him around his body (see Figure 13.1)

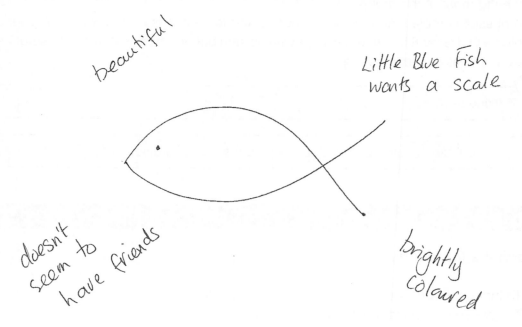

Figure 13.1

Hot seating the teacher in role: meeting Rainbow Fish

Explain that all of the creatures are going to have the chance to tell Rainbow Fish some of the things they have been talking about and perhaps how they feel about him. Say that some of the creatures may want to be friends or some may want to ask him questions. Tell the children that in this activity you will be Rainbow Fish. Sit on a chair and try to look proud. In turn, the sea creatures go up to the chair and speak to Rainbow Fish. Rainbow fish responds appropriately:

- *They are my scales, why should I have to give them away?*
- *I am very beautiful, aren't I?*
- *The octopus said to me 'Give up your scale, it will make you happy.' I don't know whether it will. How could I be happy without them?*
- *I don't know what to do.*
- *Would you give away your scales or favourite toy to someone who asked you?*

Rainbow Fish leaves and the other creatures discuss him:

- *What is he like?*
- *What did he say?*
- *Do you think he should give his scales away?*

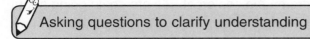 Asking questions to clarify understanding

Add detail to the role on the wall by writing what they have learned inside the body shape (see Figure 13.2)

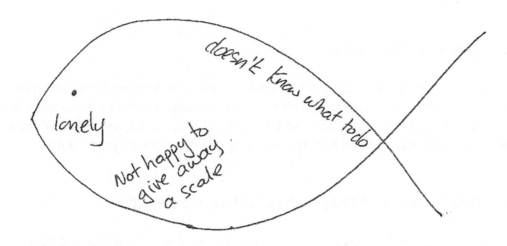

Figure 13.2

Giving advice: what should Rainbow Fish do?

Poor old Rainbow Fish is in a difficult position. Should he give his scales away or not? Ask if the children can give Rainbow Fish some advice. Children, in two lines facing each other, form a tunnel for the teacher in role as Rainbow Fish to walk down and as he passes they tell him what they think he should do.

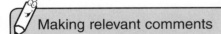 Making relevant comments

Add thought bubbles to the role on the wall indicating the advice Rainbow Fish has been given

Rainbow Fish makes his decision

Teacher's intentions

- To resolve the problem positively;
- To discuss alternative endings.

Whole-group improvisation and teacher in role: Rainbow Fish has some news

Tell the children that in the last part of the drama the sea creatures are again going about their business in the sea and you in role as Rainbow Fish will arrive to speak to them all. Rainbow Fish greets them and asks them to come and sit down for a chat. He tells them that after listening to some good advice and thinking about things he has decided to give each of them a present of one of his scales. This is not just because they are asking for one but because realizes that he wants to share with them as sharing gives him a warm feeling. It's not just about giving something away but about making someone else happy and feeling happy himself because he has made someone else happy!

Ritual: giving of the scales

Rainbow Fish asks the creatures come forward one at a time. He 'gives' each of them a scale in a ritualistic way. This could be done with cut-out scales or the scales could be imaginary. Rainbow Fish tells them to take care of the scales, as they are special. He invites them all to his cave and hopes that they will all become good friends.

Storytelling: telling Old Grey Fish what has happened

Encourage the group to have the opportunity to think about the actions of Rainbow Fish in this story by asking them to retell the events to Old Grey Fish, who has not been there. Sit in the Old Grey Fish's chair and apologize for not having been there: perhaps be out of breath from swimming so quickly.

- *I'm amazed to see you all with scales!*
- *Please tell me how you got them.*
- *I hope you haven't stolen them from Rainbow Fish or bullied him in to giving them away.*

They explain what had happened. Perhaps probe further to ask how they feel.

- *Do they feel sorry for him?*
- *Have they been unkind?*

 Discussion, explore ideas and feelings

Reflection: what have we learned?

Discuss the dilemma of the story with the children.

- *Was it right that Rainbow Fish felt he had to give away his scales?*
- *Is there a moral to this story?*
- *What do they think would have happened if he had decided to keep them?*
- *What makes a good friend?*

Discuss the drama that they have done. Can they remember the sequence of activities?

 Comment on the drama in which they have taken part

Read the *Rainbow Fish* or other *Rainbow Fish* books by Marcus Pfister

Make a display of the books

Add scales to the role on the wall with the name of your best friend and a sentence saying why 'Lia is my best friend cos she's nice ...'

Make individual or group rainbow fish and write ideas on scales indicating what makes a good friend

Chapter 14
Pierre the Rabbit

Pierre the French lop rabbit is not very happy. He is different from all the other rabbits and animals that live with Aunt Mary on her farm. He is very shy and lacks confidence. Can the children reassure him that although we are all different, we all have something to offer?

Learning objectives

- To understand that we are all different;
- Diversity and inclusion;
- Pets.

Resources

- Optional props for Pierre – furry gloves, coat.

Notes

In this drama the teacher has two different roles, Aunt Mary and Pierre the rabbit. Please don't act like a rabbit! You are taking on the role not the animal characteristics so no hopping or nose twitching is required. The role as it is written does suggest a French accent, but could be done without.

What are your favourite pets?

Teacher's intentions

- Sharing knowledge and understanding of how to care for animals.

Discussion: our pets

Children sit in a circle. Tell them that the story they are going to tell today is about a pet. Ask the children to think about their own pets and or which animal they would like to have if they were able to have one. Talk about the positive aspects of keeping animals as pets and also the negative ones.

Sharing information; listing

Draw simple pictures of pets and write a list onto a large sheet of paper

Game: listening and sequencing

Play the cumulative circle game 'My Aunt Mary went shopping and she bought a cat, a cat and a dog, a cat and a dog and a goldfish ...' Children are asked to offer one new pet to the list on each turn. Pictures of pets could be pulled out of a bag and stuck on the wall to remind children of the sequence.

Sequencing; taking turns

Write out the list of animals with supporting pictures

Mime and improvisation: we've all got pets

Ask children to pretend they are going to be holding one of the pets, e.g. the cat. Give running commentary of what you are doing and encourage children to join in with you.

- *Here's my cat, Sandy. I'm going to pick him up/put him on my lap. Come on Sandy ...* [Pretend to pick up the cat carefully, show the size and weight of the cat with your hands.]
- *What's your cat's name?* [Ask children to share names. Comment such as *'Oh, that's a lovely name! What a fine name for a cat!'*]

Describe your cat and encourage children to describe theirs. Practice holding, feeding, and grooming your pet and encourage the children to copy you and develop their own ideas. Respond to the children's contributions and use them to shape the direction of the activity.

- *Sandy likes to eat tuna fish. What does your cat like?*
- *What should we do now?*
- *Does he need to go for a rest in his basket?*
- *Don't brush him too hard!*
- *Does he like to be tickled on this tummy or under his chin, like this?*

Ask children to introduce their pet to a partner and tell each other something about their pet. This could be repeated for other animals with different characteristics, e.g. dogs need taking for a walk – they sometimes run off and need to be called and caught, their 'poop' needs to be scooped, they often go in ponds and need to be bathed ...

 Responding to what they have heard with relevant comments, actions or questions. Extending vocabulary. Speaking clearly and with confidence. Show an awareness of the listeners

> Write a list of instructions for how to look after a pet. Write a list of requirements such as: a pet needs exercise, food, water, company and somewhere to sleep. Draw an annotated picture of a pet indicating its name, favourite food, favourite games

Freeze frame: pose for the camera!

Ask the children to pose individually or as a whole group so you can take 'a photograph' of them with their pets.

Ask open and closed questions to individual children by 'tapping' them on the shoulder.

- *What do you like about your pet?*
- *What is his name?*
- *What does she like to eat?*
- *How do you keep her coat looking so shiny?*

> Answering questions; including relevant detail
>
> Description, vocabulary extension, asking and answering questions, using talk to clarify thinking, using phonic knowledge to write simple regular words

> Children draw a picture of themselves with their pet. It can be labeled

Aunt Mary has a problem

Teacher's intentions

- To introduce the teacher in role and the problem.

Teacher in role: discovering the problem

Tell the children that you are going to tell a story about someone called Aunt Mary who has a problem with her pet and that you are going to pretend to be her. Ask them whether they will be happy to help Aunt Mary. Perhaps use a prop to indicate when you are in role – a hat or scarf. Make it clear that the story has started by walking away and then coming back to the group looking worried. Aunt Mary is a bit silly. She is very caring but incapable of looking after her pet but doesn't realize it.

Hello everyone. I'm Mary – everybody calls me Aunt Mary. I have heard that you are all very caring people who love animals and know how to look after pets. I have got lots of animals living with me on my farm: chickens, geese, pigs and some rabbits and I am very excited because I have just bought myself a new pet rabbit. He is a special type called a French Lop rabbit and he's called Pierre. Oh dear! It's not working out very well so far and I'm very worried about him. He's very grouchy and acting strangely. I don't know what the matter is. I don't know what to do. Do you think I'm looking after him properly?

Encourage the children to ask you questions about your rabbit and how you are looking after him (food, water, bedding, exercise, company). Listen to all the advice; prompt them to ask questions when necessary. Reassure the children you are doing all of these things to keep him fit and healthy but perhaps realize there is one thing you are not doing as well as you could, e.g. he might need more exercise or more water. Give them answers based on the information here. French lop rabbits:

- have long ears – 20–38cm long;
- are large and heavy with wide heads;
- are usually good tempered;
- eat fresh hay, dry rabbit mix and fresh fruit and vegetables;
- are intelligent and responsive;
- like to live with a companion;
- if they live alone and don't get regular exercise can become depressed and antisocial.

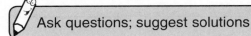

Ask questions; suggest solutions

Research French lop rabbits

Draw and label French lop rabbits, showing their special characteristics

Meeting Pierre

Teacher's intentions

- To develop empathy;
- To raise the issue of inclusion;
- To solve the problem.

Teacher in role: Pierre shares his worries

Tell the children that Aunt Mary was really please to have had a chat with them and that she took their advice about (giving more exercise/more food). Unfortunately, Pierre is still not very happy. Aunt Mary was wondering whether they could have a chat to him and see whether he'll tell them why he is unhappy.

Confirm that the children know that they need to be sympathetic when talking to someone who is upset. Discuss how they can approach Pierre and what kind of questions they could ask him.

Tell the children that you will pretend to be Pierre. Perhaps have a bag with a few props inside which you can wear/use to represent the rabbit. Let the children see you and help you to put the items on.

Teacher in role as Pierre meets the children.

Bonjour everyone. Hello everyone. Je m'appelle Pierre – my name is Pierre. That's Peter in English. Comment ça va? How are you?

Encourage the children to ask you questions to discover what the matter is. Don't give all the answers away too quickly. Pierre should eventually tell the children his problem:

Je pense que ... I think that the other rabbits don't like me. They say I am different from them. They say I have a funny accent. They say I have long silly ears. They laugh at me. Je pense que they don't like me. They call me nasty names. They are not friendly. It makes me sad.

Can the children reassure Pierre and suggest what he could do? Are the rabbits jealous of his long ears and accent? Is it just because he is different? Could he talk to Aunt Mary? Is there one rabbit that seems friendlier than the others who he could talk to? See what solutions the children provide, but avoid confrontations and violence as you are a very peaceful rabbit who does not want to behave badly.

 Responding sensitively; making suggestions

Narration and letter: things get better

Finish the story by narrating what happens to Pierre when he returns to the farm. Pierre uses some of the children's suggestions and eventually feels better. The other rabbits may not have miraculous change of heart but Pierre shows them that he is the same as they are inside and gradually things improve. Perhaps he could teach them some French?

The children receive a letter from Pierre thanking them for their help (Figure 14.1).

> Bonjour children!
>
> *Comment ça va?* How are you? *J'ai très joli aujourd'hui.* I am very happy today, *parce que* I have some new friends. Thank you for giving me such good help. *Je pense que* I will like living here at Tante Marie's farm now. Please come and visit me soon.
>
> Love
>
> Pierre xxx

Figure 14.1

 Reading, translating, responding to text

Write a reply to Pierre

Reflection: what have we learned?

Discuss the story. Recap on the reasons for Aunt Mary's concerns and Pierre's sadness and how they helped them to solve their problems.

- *How is Pierre different?*

- *Does this matter?*
- *Should Aunt Mary have bought a pet without knowing how to look after it?*
- *Do all animals need the same care?*
- *Can they remember any French words?*

Perhaps go on to discuss the way this story relates to the children's own lives, if appropriate.

Sustaining active listening, asking questions, responding sensitively, offering advice

Show an understanding of the elements of stories, characters, sequences of events

Retell the story of Pierre in a story circle, sequencing events and adding detail

Draw a picture and write captions about Pierre when he was sad and Pierre when he was happier. Pierre was sad because … Pierre is happy because …

Can the children answer the questions Where? Who? Why? How? about this story?

Compile a simple English–French dictionary, focusing on animals

Recommended Reading

Baldwin, P. (2004) *With Drama in Mind: Real Learning in Imagined Worlds*. Stafford: Network Educational Press.

Baldwin, P. (2008) *The Practical Primary Drama Handbook*. London: Paul Chapman.

Baldwin, P. and Fleming, K. (2002) *Teaching Literacy through Drama: Creative Approaches*. London: Routledge Falmer.

Boulton, J. & Ackroyd, J. (2004) *Role Play in the early Years: The Teddy Bears' Picnic and other stories*. David Fulton Publishers.

Boulton, J. & Ackroyd, J. (2004) *Role Play in the early Years: Pirates and other Adventures*. David Fulton Publishers.

Boulton, J. & Ackroyd, J. (2004) *Role Play in the early Years: The Toymaker's Workshop and other tales*. David Fulton Publishers.

Bowell, P. and Heap, B. (2001) *Planning Process Drama*. London: David Fulton Publishers.

Clipson-Boyles, S. (2011) *Teaching Primary English through Drama: A practical and creative Approach*. David Fulton Books.

Dickinson, R. and Neelands, J. (2006) *Improve your Primary School through Drama*. London: David Fulton.

Farmer, D. (2011) *Learning Through Drama in the Primary Years*. Drama Resource.

Miller, C. and Saxton, J. (2004) *Into the Story: Language in Action Through Drama*. Heinemann; Portsmouth, NH.

Saxton, J. and Miller, C.S. (2004) *Into the Story: Language in Action Through Drama*. Portsmouth, New Hampshire: Heinemann.

Tandy, M. (2010) *Creating Drama with 4–7 Year Olds: Lesson Ideas to Integrate Drama into the Primary Curriculum*. London: Routledge

Toye, N. and Prendiville, F. (2000) *Drama and Traditional Story for the Early Years*. London: Routledge.

Winston, J. (2004) *Drama and English at the Heart of the Curriculum: Primary and Middle Year*. London: David Fulton

Winston, J. and Tandy, M. (2008) *Beginning Drama 4–11 (Early Years & Primary)*. London: David Fulton.

Winston, J. and Tandy, M. (2012) *Beginning Shakespeare 4–11* London: Routledge.

Woolland, B. (2010) *Teaching Primary Drama*. Harlow: Pearson Longman.